Praise for *Poems, Piety, and*

"David Keighley probes beneath the surfa⸺ ⸺ ⸺ and provides us with a basis for believing in our troubled world. So long as we have people like David, Christianity will live and renew itself."

—John Shelby Spong, former Bishop of Newark, and author of *Why Christianity Must Change or Die*

"This volume of poetry is a true treasure. Poems are words so twisted and so pressed that they express the matter more densely and subtly than if they were left to their own devices. Poetry takes a handful of words and turns them into a discourse of desire—of longing, lament, and laughter. Poetry twists words into new shapes and ideas that add to our very being. Good poems create something out of nothing. Poetry is always greater than the sum of its parts. David Keighley's poems have a beauty and sincerity about them that sound the depths, soothe the soul, and touch the heavens."

—Martyn Percy, Dean of Christ Church, University of Oxford, and author of *Power and the Church*

"Having watched David minister to far-flung congregations of mostly elderly parishioners in ancient stone churches, I was aware of his frustrations as he tried to communicate the essence of Christ's teachings, sans the institutional bureaucracy and dogma that can obscure the message of love, compassion, and forgiveness. David's poetry, refined, yet painfully raw, lays bare his innermost feelings about the ossification of what should be the Living Word. When I think of how courageous Jesus was when he spoke out against the hypocrisy of established Judaism, I have a feeling that if he were here now, Jesus would be blasting out David's poems on all his social media streams, hoping that readers would be compelled to rise up, speak truth to power, and save Christianity."

—Kathy Eldon, author of *Soul Catcher*

"In his poetry, David has found his voice as a confident doubter, an example of the person of faith who, in growing older, believes less and less, and yet believes what he does believe more and more. David's critique of woodenly literal readings of Scripture and received doctrine is part of this. But it's not the armchair assault of the detached intellectual. There's a ruthless self-questioning in these poems, an examination of the foundations of his faith, even a willingness to interrogate his own vocation as a priest and ask what it has all been about. It feels challenging at times, even painful, to overhear this inner conversation. But this journey is necessary, I think, not only for David but for all of us if we are to have integrity as people of faith in a world of bewildering (yet beautiful) complexity. In such a world, religion can only ever be not the answer but the question. I'm grateful to David's poems for helping me understand that more clearly."

—Michael Sadgrove, Dean Emeritus of Durham, and author of *Christ in a Choppie Box*

"David has a wonderful propensity for saying so much in only a few words: a single short poem can sum up an entire theology. I am delighted that he is sharing his special gifts in this new book. It's a winner and a keeper!"

—William Aulenbach, retired Episcopal priest, and author of *Cramming for the Finals: New Ways of Looking at Old Church Ideas*

"I am not a particularly religious person, but David's take on Christianity is so refreshing and vital. Times are changing fast, and we must all keep up or risk being left behind. David refuses to be left behind, fighting to bring the relevant and purest form of Christianity back into our lives. Forget the myths, the lies, the hell, and damnation, and find the truth. It's simpler than you think, and David's poems will point you in the right direction."

—Sarah Parish, actress and television personality, and co-founder of Murray Parish Trust

"I am thrilled to bits by this collection of poems. They are courageous and so very honest. They speak so plainly, but in their few words, and often with a sharp wit, conjure up such large questions for us all to consider—especially those of us who call ourselves Christians.... These are important poems for the church to hear, and I hope they will find a wide audience both inside it and amongst those who have given it up for lost. We all need to think again, and again, and again."

—Trevor Dennis, former Tutor in Old Testament Studies, Salisbury and Wells Theological College

"David Keighley's word grenades—they aren't quite verses—provoke and prod: What's God? These gobbets of questing doubt are a lot more interesting than any virtual mass from an archbishop's kitchen."

—Quentin Letts, journalist, writer, critic, and broadcaster

"David Keighley, fellow priest, pilgrim, and (re)searcher. His work shines a light into those dark recesses of the church and those parts of its preposterous theology, which it would rather remain in the dark."

—David Jenkins, Professor Emeritus of Theology, Leeds University, and author of *God, Miracle and the Church of England*

"David became a wise and dear friend through his work with troubled minds rather than troubled souls. His poetry reveals to us how inextricably bound up in each other they are. To lose yourself in his words is to find the good or God in a phrase or a verse that soothes both. Thank you David for your sincerity, courage, and energy."

—Rebecca Hardy, *Daily Mail* journalist

Poems, Piety, and Psyche

Dear Sybil,
with many thanks for
the years of friendship
x support!
x
David

Poems, Piety, and Psyche

Progressive Poems for Rebellious Christians

David John Keighley

RESOURCE *Publications* · Eugene, Oregon

POEMS, PIETY, AND PSYCHE
Progressive Poems for Rebellious Christians

Resource Publications
An Imprint of Wipf and Stock Publishers
199 W. 8th Ave., Suite 3
Eugene, OR 97401

www.wipfandstock.com

PAPERBACK ISBN: 978-1-7252-8071-7
HARDCOVER ISBN: 978-1-7252-8070-0
EBOOK ISBN: 978-1-7252-8072-4

Manufactured in the U.S.A.   10/21/20

For Sally, Spong, and Sheldon
To Sally, the best spouse and clergy wife ever
My fantastic children:
Hannah
Paul
Emily
Lucy

In Memoriam:
Doreen Keighley (1923–2015)
Howard, C P-H and David

Jack Spong, for his encouragement, inspired teaching,
and friendship;
Sheldon, for their courageous ministry and clergy care;
and the people of Lanlivery in Cornwall.

A donation to the Murray-Parish Trust, dedicated to the
advancement of pediatric emergency medicine across southern
England and investing in ground-breaking research into childhood
illness, will be made on the sale of each volume.

MURRAY
PARISH
TRUST

Advancing Paediatric Emergency Medicine
"Making sure our children get the best possible care"

Contents

Acknowledgments

Jan Moran Neil, my poetry tutor with a red pen. Sandy Draper, for dealing so expertly with the copyediting. Adrian House and Sarah Parish, for the years of theological exploration. Caroline Harvie, Verna Roberts, Caroline and Peter Hobson, my critical friends for their "views from the pews." George Callihan, Zechariah Mickel, Caleb Shupe, Savanah N. Landerholm, and the team at Wipf and Stock, for their professional guidance from the start, and Shannon Carter for her stunning cover design. Michael Sadgrove, who started me on this path at theological college. Finally, my tolerant wife, Sally, who lost me to my writing cabin for so many hours.

Preface

Forty years ago, as a member of a group of clever theological students, we visited a famous advertising firm in London, J. Walter Thomson. Being clever, we asked how they would "market the Church of England." After some serious consideration, their executives produced their answer, "Change the product." It would seem today, after all these years, that the "product" is still not very marketable.

The packaging has changed, however, if you look closely. A modified Liturgy, the introduction of new services, catchy new hymns, entertaining children with "messy church," providing coffee stations, employing "outreach" consultants, and so on—but under the packaging, the product is still the same. Believers are still expected to believe the unbelievable and suspend rational thought.

The church has been unable to absorb the teaching of Biblical criticism, the reality of evolution, the false idea of a God "up there," and accept that Christianity must adapt and incorporate these ideas, just as any scientifically educated twelve-year-old does. There is, in my poems, an emphasis on the teaching of the historical Jesus while rejecting the miracles of the virgin birth or his physical resurrection. Jesus was Divine in the sense that we see God in him in the same way—though to a greater degree—as in the lives of all holy men and women, and each other, if we look closely enough.

The social issues of the day are equally avoided by the church as it still battles with how human beings manage their relationships. Second marriages, female priests and bishops, sex outside marriage, and the LGBTQ community continue to occupy the minds of church authorities, as the population walks on by without a glance in their direction.

Congregations have been duped into perpetuating "it really did happen," which has buried Christ under myth, magic, and make-believe. University theology faculties are not so taken in, but churches are so influenced by traditional teachings, which encourages literalism. Hence the decline of the church in today's world, as the next generation—fresh from the tea-towel experience of the nativity play—tends to ditch their faith as soon as they arrive at their teen years. This is the generation gap we see in our churches, which are acknowledged by decline—in numbers, clergy, and cash, and it is this my poems attempt to address.

I am no academic theologian. My theological exploration has been that of a country parson for nearly four decades. Theology on the hoof. Coping day by day with the needs, trials, and tribulations of God's "people in the street." This doesn't stop me from having my theological heroes—such as Bishop John Robinson, Don Cupitt, Bishop David Jenkins, the American Bishop Jack Spong, to name a few. Brave ordinary priests, also theologians whose thoughts and writings have been criticized and vilified and whose careers have been blighted, like Jeffrey John and Anthony Freeman. Some of whom have received poison-pen letters (anonymous naturally) and death threats for their beliefs and thinking. Beliefs that their church has dismissed, not considered, explored, or accepted. Sometimes with violence, always with disdain and inevitably, with anger.

A company is only as good as its board of directors. It is no good claiming the authority of leadership and then failing to deliver the goods—the shareholders would not be impressed. Those who have run and overseen church life—the bench of bishops, over the years—should hang their heads in shame at their public adherence of the literal interpretation of the Christian Gospel, while privately believing the opposite. Theological colleges have made clergy complicit in this by maintaining the myths of Christianity as literal, and it is why, over the past forty years, we have lost a generation, who are now non-believers. Hardworking parish priests struggling to run multiple parishes, increased administration, demands of diocesan initiatives, and paperwork have lost the imperative which used to be the foundation of parish ministry—"A house-going priest makes a churchgoing people." The collapse of support for parish priests suffering emotional conditions and serious mental distress due to the dedicated service to their people, who frequently are the cause of this suffering, adds another cause to the declining condition of today's church. Far from being a tower of strength to their workforce, the ecclesiastical hierarchy is proving to be contributory to the emotional suffering of the clergy and their families. You only have to read the stories on clergy support organizations, like the Sheldon community in Devon, to realize how damaging the whole system has become.

The Christian story taken literally does not happen in the "generation gaps" scientific, postmodern world. Stars do not stop over maternity wards where unhygienic shepherds visit with their sheep while listening to heavenly choirs. As adults, these people lead satisfying lives, untouched by faith, God, or Jesus. They walk past the church, immune to the noise coming from within about the status of women and human sexuality. They see the frantic activity of events to raise yet more money to prop up buildings and an institution—as if God needs money! It is all irrelevant to them. They don't believe a word. It is all our fault, and not another Diocesan Bishop's Initiative (I have endured five now) will set things right or find the formula to fill the churches. How do these initiatives expect to "lead the Church into growth" when the people see no reason to be led in that direction?

At school assemblies for four decades, after reading a passage of scripture, I would ask, not "did it happen?" but "what does it mean?" The fact the scripture is written in such a way that the reader, especially the young reader, is expected to take it literally does not clarify the real intention of the Gospel writers. So I appreciate that to the academic theologian, my poems may be a little naive. However, the academic theologian already understands the "meaning behind the miracles." I write for the person in the street who should be sitting in the pew.

An angry tone may seem to run through these poems. I think that is true, as I am angry about the things which have contributed to the decline of my church and world in my lifetime: inadequate teaching and an education system focused on facts rather than how to live a contented and fulfilled life; the literal interpretations of unbelievable religious history; poor leadership; sex scandals and toxic church leaders; the contamination of young, idealistic minds with dangerously manipulative ideas; the general sense that the church remains out of touch with normal people over issues of sexuality and the role of women, despite all the brave words trying to remedy that impression. If you are not angry in today's world, there is something wrong with you. Poverty, child abuse, failing educational systems, domestic violence, religious terrorism, environmental damage, excessive wealth, rampant consumerism, rogue states, egomaniac world leaders, political hypocrisy—just how long a list do you want?

These poems are post-modern progressive Christianity with a rebellious tone, and their purpose is simple: demythologize much of Christian theology; challenge the literalism of doctrine and scriptures; and disclose the still valid, hidden truths. It is my disillusionment that motivates me to write. My words are offered as a small corrective to the unknowing of church believers, and those outside the church, who deserve better. I fully expect to join my heroes and be ignored, and like them, I do believe. I believe in creation (who can't believe in creation?) and in the Christ, whose message of agape for the world can't be ignored and for which the world is in desperate need.[1]

David Keighley
Meonstoke, Hampshire, UK
davidkeighleywriter.com
July 2020

1. I am writing the final few poems in this anthology during the lockdown phase of the pandemic. As I reflect on the situation the world finds itself in, I am more determined than ever to continue writing in the tone of this anthology. As I re-read the last sentence of this Preface, I appreciate fully now that the essence of agape is "universalizability"—the universal love of God for all humankind. This universal love has not yet achieved its potential, but in this pandemic, we see it in action globally. As doctors, nurses, medical staff, carers, delivery drivers, street cleaners, food producers and supermarket workers, and the list goes on, are all working to meet the needs of suffering humanity regardless of race, gender, color, religion, wealth, sexual orientation, or any of the other categories of discrimination usually in daily use. Only the selfish, the stockpilers of goods, those ignoring social separation guidelines, threaten this universal love through their ignorance. The rest of us are coming together to address the desperate human need the world is experiencing. The best of humankind coming out in this pandemic is exactly the "universalizability' of Christianity, which I write about in an attempt to recover for the "lost generation," which is in danger of missing out due to the fundamentalist and traditional teaching of the church. A church that will surely die if it doesn't change.

PART I

Creation and Bible Stories

Horses for Courses

Are we made in his image,
or is it the other way round?

Where was God before humankind's
words and concepts and ideas?

They say if horses had a god,
He would be a horse.

Leaving Home[1]

I'm off!

I must leave behind the political and ethical compromises that have corrupted the faith of my Jesus.

I must leave the stifling theology, the patriarchal structures.

I must leave the enduring prejudices based on our God-given humanity,

the color of my skin, my gender, or how my sexual orientation is practiced.

I must leave the mentality that encourages anyone to think our doctrines are unchangeable.

I must leave the belief of those who believe our sacred texts are without error.

I must leave the God of miracle and magic.

I must leave behind the promises of certainty, the illusion of possessing the true faith.

I must leave the claims of being the recipient of an unchallengeable revelation.

I must leave the neurotic religious desire to know that I am right and to play at being God.

I must leave the claim that every other pathway to God is second-rate, that fellow Hindu searchers in India, Buddhists in China and Tibet, Muslims in the Middle East, and the Jews of Israel are inadequate.

I must leave the pathway that tells me all other directions will get me lost.

I must leave the certain claim that my Jesus is the only way to God for everyone.

I must leave the ultimate act of human folly that says it is.

I must leave my church, my home.

I must leave behind my familiar creeds and faith symbols

I can no longer stay in an unlivable place.

I must move to where I can once again sing the Lord's song.

I must move to where my faith tradition can be revived and live on.

I must move to where children don't tell me what I believe is unbelievable, but tell me they can believe what I believe.

1. For Bishop Jack Spong, 2007.

I must move to where they are not just playing at moving the chairs on the decks of an ecclesiastical *Titanic*.

I can never leave the God experience.
I can never walk away from the doorway into the Divine that I believe I have found in the one I call "the Christ" and acknowledge as "my Lord."
I must move to dangerous and religiously threatening places.
I must move where there is no theism, but still God.

I must be off—to God knows where.

Deadwood

God would, as any gardener would,
cut out the deadwood.
But Eden is perfect,
creation complete.
Divine gardener can rest content.

Man and Woman made after tea break,
to live in the luxury of perfection
with every need met.

Except one—
forbidden fruit to stay untouched
to save from knowing good from evil.
Temptation too much for mortals
and Paradise is lost.

Shame and Guilt arrive,
and fig leaves save blushes.
Why are genitals sinful and not elbows or feet?
How did they know what to cover?
Did God point and say, "I don't like that bit, it's naughty?"

"It's her fault," said Adam,
in what would become man's universal cry.
But the gates of Eden loom
beneath an angelic sword
and the snake forever slithers,
which doesn't seem much of a punishment—
for a snake.

Man finds himself suddenly in need,
of saving from original sin,

saving from his human nature,
if he is to regain happiness.
God, getting over his disappointment,
decides to help pathetic humanity.

Humankind was in serious need of rescue from itself.

Seven[2]

"God called the light 'Day,' and the darkness he called 'Night';
and there was evening, and there was morning—the first day."

"Young Earth," creationists say,
four thousand years ago
God made the world,
including dinosaurs, *creatio ex nihilo,* with all the other animals.
But Satan planted their bones in the mud
to deceive Homo sapiens,
and lead them away from the true faith.

"God called the dome 'Sky';
and there was evening, and there was morning—the second day."

Conveniently dismissing radioactive carbon dating
the creationists' time fails to acknowledge a period
sixty-five to 230 million years ago,
when dinosaur bones got stuck in the mud to become fossils.
Creationist time doesn't go that far back.

"God called the dry land 'Earth,' and the waters he called 'Seas.'
Then God said, 'Let the earth put forth vegetation';
and there was evening, and there was morning—the third day."

The Creationists' Bible is true
and all the stories really happened.
Two by two, all the dinosaurs went on board
what must have been an enormous boat indeed,
even though the Bible records its size—in feet.
Or maybe Noah collected eggs or baby dinosaurs?

2. "These are the generations of the heavens and the earth when they were created,"
Genesis, 1–2.

"God made the two great lights—the greater light to rule the day
and the lesser light to rule the night—and the stars;
and there was evening, and there was morning—the fourth day."

Perhaps, they say, the dinosaurs missed the boat
and drowned with all the other extinct species,
and were not wiped out after the cretaceous period.
Thank goodness we have crocodiles
to remind us they were real,
Oh, and the Loch Ness monster.

"God made great sea monsters and every living creature that moves, of every
kind,
with which the waters swarm, and every winged bird of every kind;
and there was evening, and there was morning—the fifth day."

Creationists hope they might find a dinosaur one day,
perhaps in the rainforests of South America.
This would show those scientists up
and rubbish the theory of evolution and their scientific ways,
not knowing that this would prove nothing of the sort.
Evolution happily believes in isolated survival,
remember the Coelacanth, thought extinct,
turning up in the 1930s?
Scientists would relish finding T-rex in the jungle
to get at its DNA,
and show its evolutionary fellowship with birds.

"God made the wild animals of the earth of every kind, then God said,
'Let us make humankind in our image; and there was evening, and there was
morning—the sixth day."

Clutching at straws now,
they tell us dinosaurs are in the Bible,
where they are called "dragons"—fearsome, scaly creatures,

conveniently ignoring that the human race
didn't turn up until ten million years later.
Explains why there are no cave paintings of T-rex.
Paleontologists hand this one over to the theologians.
Let them go on burning the books on evolution,
but let the children choose.
And it's no good trying the "intelligent design creationism" either.
We are on to that.

"And on the seventh day, God finished the work that he had done,
and he rested on the seventh day from all the work that he had done in
creation."

A pity Science and Faith have become enemies,
and Young Earth Creationists
can't find it in themselves to toss out their Bibles,
or take lessons from theologians,
and interpret it allegorically or as a symbol.
And so, they suffer self-inflicted anguish and pain
in their delusional world.

In the Beginning

If God made the world,
and Adam and Eve next,
who cuddled,
or ate an apple sinfully,
in the Garden of Eden?

And before Noah's Ark and all the animals,
including the dinosaurs,
floated off the mountain
and everybody else drowned,
except for the fish,
leaving Noah's family to populate the Earth
under a rainbow,
then, why, by now:

Haven't we stopped believing the unbelievable?
And start to have doubts about all that follows?
And wonder why anybody would put these stories first
if they were trying to convince us it was all true?

Myths,
which, after all, tell the truth
told at the beginning could be a clue to future reading,
maybe?

The Apple

Augustine has a lot to answer for.
He admits to sexual hang-ups,
a lascivious life,
then celibate,
but ends up shaping
how Christians view sex.
How did that happen?

He tells us the physical act between men and women
is the root and origin of sin—
the sin of Adam and Eve.
Eve's desire for the forbidden apple
revealed her debauchery,
her sin of sexual desire and passion.

Why the blush at God-given out-of-control genitals?
The horror at their future sighting,
which demands fig leaves
to cover maidens' shame,
and hold the corruption of his accursed seed.

Now all men are cursed
from the beginning,
passed on from one man's sin
spoiling the fun for evermore;
as punishment,
by which the devil can control us.

Why did God instruct his first-made creatures
to be fruitful and people the Earth?
And risk sinful passion passing to our children across the ages?
Except for Mary and Joseph,

a special case,
where Christ's flesh was formed in a virgin womb,
not when making children.

"The perfect Christian couple live together as brother and sister."
"Self-willed passion in the sexual organs is caused by sin."
Augustine really has a lot to answer for.

Why did the sex police have to make Magdalene a prostitute?
Magdalene, Jesus's favorite disciple,
the "one most loved."

Augustine has more to answer for than he ever realized,
planting his sexual timebomb for our generation.

Freud would have loved them as patients.

Wrong Saying

We use the phrase "theory of evolution,"
to bring us confidently to this conclusion,
that Darwinism
is a fact,
an actuality,
a certainty,
authentic,
has existence,
and certitude,
with
cold,
hard,
evidence.

Evolution is not a theory.
It explains the mystery
of our history.

Creationists are faced with anachronism
and speculation,
a guess,
a hunch,
a surmise,
an opinion,
a hypothesis,
when trying to authenticate
their belief that God did it all.

Creationism is a theory,
which is contrary to our ancestry
and is unable to accommodate
a view that is not legitimate.

Creationism is a theory.
Evolution is not a theory,
because carbon dating is quite convincing.

God Is Dead[3]

Nietzsche didn't mean God had actually died,
but that humankind had killed him, dissatisfied
with the view that Divine Providence
made more sense than Science.

If God sent Jesus to show us how to live
and now *"God is Dead"* is the graffiti narrative,
and Morality is now our choice,
no longer imposed from on high,
Do we just have to get on with it,
freed of guidelines from the sky?

3. "God is dead," Nietzsche, 1882.

67 Miracles

Creation of the Universe, including plants, animals and humans;
this one takes some beating.

The flood of Noah.

The confusion of tongues and languages.

Destruction of Sodom and Gomorrah.

Lot's wife turned into a pillar of salt.

Sarah and Abraham conceive a child Isaac in their old age.

The burning bush not consumed.

The miracle of Aaron's rod changed into a serpent.

The ten plagues of Egypt: water becomes blood, frogs, lice, flies, murrain, boils, thunder and hail, locusts, darkness,
death of the first-born.

The miracle of the Red Sea parted.

God answers Moses's prayer for water in the wilderness.

Manna from heaven.

Moses smites the rock and water came out.

Fire devours Nadab and Abihu.

Some of the people consumed by fire at Taberah.

The earth opens and swallows up Korah and his company.

Fire from the Lord consumes 250 at Kadesh.

The plague at Kadesh slays 14,700 for murmuring against Moses.

The miracle of Aaron's rod budding at Kadesh.

Water from the rock, smitten twice by Moses in the desert of Zin.

The brazen serpent heals the people bitten by the fiery serpents.

Balaam's donkey speaks.

The Jordan parts so that Israel passed over dry-shod near the city of Adam.

The walls of Jericho fall down.

The sun and moon stayed still to allow the Israelites to avenge their enemies.

A hailstorm destroys the enemy of the Israelites.

The Spirit of the Lord gives Samson supernatural strength.

The Lord provides Samson water from a donkey's jaw.

Dagon falls twice before the ark.

Emerods (tumors) befall the Philistines

More than 50,000 men of Beth-shemesh killed by the Lord for looking into the ark.

Thunderstorm causes a panic among the Philistines at Eben-ezer.

The Lord responds to Samuel's request with thunder and rain in the harvest at Gilgal.

The Lord creates a sound in the mulberry trees as a sign to attack the Philistines.

The Lord kills Uzziah for touching the Ark at Perez-Uzzah.

King Jeroboam's hand withered to get him to repent.

King Jeroboam's new altar destroyed at Bethel.

Miracle of Elijah and the widow's oil increase.

Miracle of Elijah and the widow's son raised from the dead.

Miracle of the drought.

Drought at Elijah's prayers.

Miracle of fire at Elijah's prayers.

Miracle of rain at Elijah's prayers.

Elijah fed by ravens.

Ahaziah's captains consumed by fire near Samaria.

Jordan divided by Elijah and Elisha near Jericho.

Elijah carried to heaven.

Waters of Jericho healed by Elisha's casting salt into them.

Elisha's curse cause bears out of the wood destroy forty-two "young men."

The Lord provides water to Jehoshaphat and the allied army.

Elisha and the Shunammite's son raised from the dead.

Elisha cures the deadly pottage.

The feeding of the hundred men with twenty loaves at Gilgal.

Naaman cured of leprosy.

The iron ax-head made to swim the River Jordan.

Elisha knows the King of Syria's plans.

Ben Hadad's plans discovered.

The Syrian army smitten with blindness at Dothan.

The Syrian army cured of blindness at Samaria.

Elisha's bones revive the dead.

God sends lions into Samaria because they did not fear the Lord.

Sennacherib's army destroyed Jerusalem.

The sun goes backward ten degrees on the sun-dial of Ahaz, Jerusalem.

Uzziah struck with leprosy.

Three Hebrew boys delivered from the fiery furnace, Shadrach, Meshach and Abed-nego.

Daniel saved in the lions' den.

Jonah safe in the belly of the whale.

The sign was given from Gideon's fleece.

Maybe not literal truths of supernatural events,

but rather ancient wisdom to indicate meaning behind a story.

Stupid! Who Me?

My six-year wise son told me,
"Vicar at assembly said you didn't have to believe it, Dad.
You don't have to believe it happened.
It's what it means that matters, not what it says."

Why didn't he tell me what it means?
In those days when I believed what they said?

When I used to go to where they said it,
and listen to them not telling us what they knew,
but we didn't,
as if we were stupid,
or not safe to know their secrets.

I do know that when Lot's wife was turned into a pillar of salt,
she didn't become a lump of sodium chloride.
I know it means not to look back in life.
I'm not that stupid.
So why won't they tell us what it means,
rather than expecting us to believe it happened?

But why, when a brave priest tells what it means,
and why it didn't happen,
are they sacked or ridiculed?
But I can still love the Lord as much as the next man,
even if I only know what it says.
Even if I don't know what it means.
Even if I don't believe it.
Even if they do still treat me as if I am stupid.
I know it's not stupid to love.

37 Miracles

Turn water into wine.

Heal an Official's son.

Drive out an evil spirit.

Heal Peter's mother-in-law.

Heal the evening sick.

Miraculous catch of fish.

Cleanse a man with leprosy.

Heal a centurion's servant.

Heal a paralytic.

Heal a man's withered hand.

Raise a widow's son in Nain.

Calm a storm.

Cast demons into a herd of pigs.

Heal a woman in the crowd.

Raise Jairus's daughter to life.

Heal two blind men.

Heal a man unable to speak.

Heal an invalid at Bethesda.

Feed 5000 people.

Walk on water.

Heal the sick in Gennesaret.

Heal a Gentile woman's demon-possessed daughter.

Heal a deaf and dumb man.

Feed 4000 people.

Heal a blind man at Bethsaida.

Heal a man born blind.

Heal a boy with a demon.

Miracle of temple tax in a fish's mouth.

Heal a blind, mute demoniac.

Heal a crippled woman.

Heal a man with dropsy on the Sabbath.

Cleanse ten lepers.

Raise Lazarus from the dead.
Restore sight to Bartimaeus.
Wither the fig tree.
Heal a servant's severed ear.
Another miraculous catch of fish.

Gospel writers despair as Truth goes unseen,
despondent that their literary creation
with theological objective, is not appreciated,
and first Testament ignorance
mislays the key to Christological revelation.

Manna from Heaven[4]

God's generosity overflows
and humanity is provided for:
"The Earth put forth vegetation: plants yielding seed,
and fruit trees of every kind,
and trees of every kind bearing fruit with the seed in it."

Global agriculture triumphs
while man's inhumanity allows hunger,
helped by a few "Acts of God,"
droughts, and the like.

Moses fed his people with manna in the desert,
the Cana wedding saved through superabundant wine,
five loaves and two fish satisfy 5000,
seven loaves and a few small fish enough for 4000 more.

But will miracles still feed people,
when seven billion humans become ten,
outstripping the ability of God to feed the world?

Or will science have to take a hand,
bypassing the Divine Provider?

4. Genesis 1:11.

Angelology

"What is Man that You are mindful of him,
or the Son of Man that You care for him?
You made him a little lower than the angels;
You crowned him with glory and honor."

—*Hebrews 2:7*

Angels are meant to be good,
aren't they?
"On the side of the angels," we say.
Pity about Satan.

Medieval theologians asked:
"How many angels can dance on the head of a pin?"

Biblical postmen before iPhones
linking up and down,
Heaven and Earth
in a flat-earth world,
appearing in dreams
to tell God's plans—
the birth of a baby.

Supernatural beings of beauty,
round and smiling.
Drifting across paintings
in diaphanous robes.

As real as the tooth fairy,
or those hiding at the bottom of the garden,
but not as scary as aliens.

Spiritual, not supernatural at all,
an angelic nurse,
my guardian angel,
showing unconditional love,
as God would.

Angels comfort anxious humanity,
who need all the help they can get,
having been made a little lower than the angels,
and having to get by without the help of
angelic superpowers.

1 AD—Possibly?

Why no birthday in the Bible?
An important date to miss out surely,
the birth of the baby Jesus?
Plenty about what and where and who but nothing about when.
Nothing in the gospels
history is incomplete,
so theologians ride to the rescue.

It could be 6 BC to 4 BC, they say.
Not 1 AD at all.
Or, to be PC, maybe CE.
BCE, not BC.
Can't upset the other religions and the atheists,
who really aren't upset or bothered in the least.

Matthew, Mark, Luke, and John,
wrote the Gospels.
They write very late after his death,
contradict themselves,
made errors distort history and so on.

Theology, not history, was their intent.

Since Herod died in 4 BC,
he didn't hear the angels sing,
and Jesus must have been born before.
But Matthew wants to blame Herod for killing the little boys,
so he moves things around a little,
and Luke has the census of Quirinius in 6 AD,
making Jesus born that year also.

History is not always convenient when storytelling.
Especially when scholars chronicle the massacre as a myth,
designed to remind us of Pharaoh killing the Hebrew children
to save his crown.
And not, as Matthew says,
because Herod feared competition.

Historical corroboration was not a high priority
for Matthew and Luke.
But we get the meaning,
which is the important thing.

Brides of Christ[5]

St. Paul blamed women for causing disruption
in church, because of what they were wearing.

A church women's program countered this
and said their members:
"Should be able to wear whatever they want when they want,"
and men *"should control their eyes."*
And *"God has wired men this way,*
men are stimulated by visual images . . .
. . . by Divine design"?

By "Divine design" indeed!
In other words,
God has programmed men to lust over women
if they are wearing immodest clothing.
So ladies, don't follow fashion
or you will cause men to sin.
Which is not what evolutionary biology tells us.

Believe it or not,
modern man
has an exceptionally large brain,
evolved over the last 200 million years,
with which to overcome the lusts and instincts
of his primitive brain,
and so, make moral choices
and not lust over women
to cause disruption in church.

5. "Women should adorn themselves in modest apparel, with propriety and moderation, not with braided hair or gold or pearls or costly clothing, but which is proper for women professing godliness," 1 Timothy 2:9–10.

So, women follow fashion if you want,
wear braided hair,
gold and pearls,
and costly clothing,
and ignore St. Paul.

Is This "The Word of the Lord"?

"Food that includes blood requires abstention."
Let's hope my children don't need a blood transfusion.

"Having sex with a man is a detestable sin."
No point in joining LGBTQ march then.

"You won't go to heaven if you are sexually immoral."
Sex antics outside marriage will turn out confrontational.

"The husband has control over his wife's body."
The feminist movement is looking pretty groggy.

"You commit adultery if you look at a woman lustfully."
Men need to keep their eyes shut when indulging in their fantasy.

"This is my commandment that you love one another as I have loved you."
This *is* the Word of the Lord.

Genesis 9:4
Leviticus 18:22
Galatians 5:19
Corinthians 7:3
Matthew 5:28
John 15:12

PART II

Gods, Hell, and Incarnation

NoOneUpThere[6]

"Our Father who art in Heaven."

A wise, eighty-five-year-old priest once told me, *"There's NoOneUpThere."*
Strange comment for a priest, I thought,
even for an American Episcopalian one.
A fire engine had hit him and his friend on their motorcycles.
His friend was killed outright.
NoOneUpThere didn't stop it happening.

"If NoOneUpThere was letting such hideous things like this happen," he said, "I want no part of this religion."
"Worship NoOneUpThere? No way."
So I wondered. . .
Why didn't NoOneUpThere keep my mom alive, stop her cancer, zap her cells?
Why did NoOneUpThere let Susan and Joe suffer the loss of their baby Lucy?
Why did NoOneUpThere, all-powerful creator of the Universe,
send a tsunami to that exquisite sandy beach?
Why did NoOneUpThere of our faith, let the terrorist with his faith, kill and maim in our lovely cities?
NoOneUpThere's Omnipotence seems to fall short.

Does NoOneUpThere pick and choose, I wonder?
You pray for the tornado to miss your village, but what about the one it hits?
You pray for Mike to get safely home tonight on the foggy motorway,
but what of the deaths in that multiple pile-up?
Did their prayers to NoOneUpThere not work as well as yours?
Whose side is NoOneUpThere on in war?
Did NoOneUpThere hear Hitler's prayers for victory, and ignore them?

Did we create NoOneUpThere, I wonder, through fear and wonder?

6. For Revd. Dr. Bill Aulenbach, 2017.

With the first few words uttered by frightened cave dwellers gazing
at the miracle of a rising sun after the darkness.
Perhaps we make our gods in the image of something known,
like the Egyptians worshipped cats.
"Our Father who art in NoHeavenUpThere . . ."
NoOneUpThere looking down, taking care, making things better.
Just us, made in the image of NoOneUpThere,
but doing his job just the same.
Loving, caring, healing.

My wise priestly friend now uses the word "Creation" for NoOneUpThere.
A force for good everywhere in the Universe.
No gender. Not judging. No son to send.
Still creating. Still evolving. Tsunami and tornado. Just Being Creation.
"You are in me, and I am in you, may they also be in us," said Jesus, maybe.
Perhaps he also agrees there's NoOneUpThere.
Just the force of Creation and the power of Jesus in us all.
But Down Here, Now!

Dream On

"Tell the children," said the teacher,
"how God communicates."
"Before the cellphone and internet monopolized the Universe."
That should be easy, in ten minutes, I thought!

The Angel of the Lord turns up a lot in the old days
Hagar and Moses, Balaam and Gideon got the message that way
As did Zechariah and Elizabeth, Mary, and the shepherds at a later time.

Dreams were common as well.
Pharaoh had a dream, but then, so did Martin Luther King
Pharaoh dreamed of cows before BSE's early form wreaked its havoc
Martin Luther King dreamed of freedom and justice, and peace.
Joseph had a dream of corn sheaves, which upset his brothers.

Pity if your REM sleep was so deep
on awakening, God's message was forgotten.
How frustrating would that be?

Mary's Joseph gets both an angel and a dream, twice, lucky him
God obviously didn't want any confusion there.
Over the important matter of his son,
there could be no mistakes.

Eventually, God couldn't trust angels and dreams,
His messages of salvation,
He sent Jesus.
Jesus sent his Holy Spirit to double-check.
This doesn't wake you in the night,
it dwells within.
Listen hard, let eyes see, let ears hear,
sensing internal voice.

Not at all loud and God-like.

More the quiet pricking of conscience.

Pseudonym

God or Bog or Zot,
Dio or Deus or Dievs?
Europe names God.

Allah or Mungu or Llaah,
Olorun or Molimo or Chineke?
Africa names God.

Xudo or Tuhan or Than,
Shen or Bondye or Diyos?
Others name God.

Do all see the same controller of the Universe,
the same creator and ruler of all,
the infinite and transcendent supreme being,
the same object of worship?

Chronology

Where did the pressure come from
to raise the dead or walk on water?
To make wine from urn-held aqua
and make the blind see?

But divinely inspired sayings speak for themselves.
They need no embellishment.
Nor inexplicable miracle base.
No Divine signpost:
"Love your enemy."
"Turn the other cheek."
"Who will cast the first stone."
"Do not judge."

Some sayings influence the world.
Across the years.
Across eternity.
Other inspired voices tried the same,
to spread their wisdom for posterity.
Einstein postulated math and science,
Hitler spread evil,
Darwin unsettled the church,
Buddha's bag was spirituality,
Rembrandt's was painting,
Mozart's music "spoke" to us,
Shakespeare acted it out,
and Aristotle just thought thinking was enough.

Did Jesus cheat, being God,
having an advantage over merely human sayings?

Other gods in their time tried their own one-upmanship,
to exert their superiority.
Aphrodite and Athena,
Bacchus and Bellona,
Mercury and Mars.
Now all are dead and buried, but where?
No one knows the location of Mercury's resting place.
Who remembers their influence?
Their message?
Their relevance to the present?

Jesus could be lost in the fullness of time.
Another god from a time gone by.
His divinity ephemeral.
His words buried beneath a bedrock for struggling humanity.

Spaceman

Sometimes I think it very odd,
to find that I believe in God.

For man has seen with his own eyes,
there is nothing there above the skies.

I used to think that very soon
we would find something,
beyond the moon.

But travels into outer space,
still won't reveal that Divine face.

Far beyond where star lights shine
the spacetime curve of bright Einstein,
still obscures this God of mine.

But God and I are not apart.
He is here,
in my heart.

Buddha-brain

When I think of the alternatives:
Atheism,
Creationism,
Naturalism,
Nontheism,
Dualism,
Pantheism,
Materialism,
Monotheism,
Humanism,
Intellectualism,
Polytheism,
Conformism,
Reductionism,
Postmodernism,
Positivism,
and Evidentialism,
my brain starts to hurt.

"God" is such a short word,
why do they make it so complicated?

May the Force be with you.

Honest to God[7]

Most folks don't connect to God,
their life has nothing to do with him
unless Auntie Vera is dying
and rusty prayers try to intervene,
or they fail to have the desired effect
and He can get the blame.

7. Acknowledgments to Bishop John A.T. Robinson.

Brian Cox and God[8]

Brian can't find God out there in space,
his views are clear upon his face.

I get depressed watching his TV shows,
because of all the things he knows.

He goes on about space and time,
and other things that do not rhyme,
like thermodynamics and entropy.

He makes my brain hurt yet again,
I really cannot stand the pain.

Science is his life, his creed, his mind,
Man's search for God gets left behind.

With quarks, black holes, red giants and stars,
he lets us sneak a look at Mars.

A while ago our sun was God,
but that old path humankind has trod.

Now we are adrift in space,
a tiny speck seeking grace.

And in the end, his mantra's clear:
a few trillion years, we won't be here.

But don't despair his views make sense,
although they make us rather tense.

8. Apologies to Professor Brian Cox.

Life has meaning without a god,
Humans' feet upon the earth have trod.

From God, you may find yourself adrift,
but life in the moment is a gift.

Whether from God or not is up to you,
and your views on eschatology.

Naughty or Nice?

"A torch, the good teacher, or an extinguisher, the clergyman?"
— *Victor Hugo*

"If I don't do this, God will be cross."
"If I'm angry, God will be upset with me."
"If I'm nice, God will like me."
"If I'm selfish, that's wrong."
"If I prefer others, God will like that."
"If I just, just, just . . ."

Will I really burn in Hell
or am I a good person, after all?

Prayers to No God

Where would our prayers go
and what would happen to them,
if You were not there to hear them
and achieve our goals for us?

"We pray for the peoples of your world.
We pray for those affected by the recent tsunami.
We pray for Mrs. Smith having an operation today.
We pray for lots of things that are wrong in your world."

And then we go home.

Love Is . . .[9]

Theologians tell us, that God, who is Love,
is hugely different from human love.

We cannot define God,
for God is incomprehensible
and so is his love,
which is not human love but Divine love.
God's love is not based on feelings or emotions
but actions.

God's love is patient and kind, it does not envy or boast,
it is not proud nor dishonors others;
it is not self-seeking or easily angered.
And it keeps no record of wrongs.

Love is choosing the other over you,
putting their needs before yours,
placing your ego firmly in the box,
or Aquinas's *"to will the good of another"*
and the Greek's *agape,* God's unconditional love.

But if God is love why does Divine love desert us
when we feel anger or hate?

---

9. Psychological research, which tells us love is not an emotion, does show twenty-six emotions which can be facially recognized: Admiration, adoration, aesthetic appreciation, amusement, anxiety, awe, awkwardness, boredom, calmness, confusion, craving, disgust, empathetic pain, entrancement, envy, excitement, fear, horror, interest, joy, nostalgia, romance, sadness, satisfaction, sexual desire, and sympathy.

Finding God

We name God,
we call on God,
we pray to God,
we are familiar with the Word of God,
but the Word is not God.

The word *tree* is not the tree.
We know the word,
we don't know God.

What we know,
or think we know,
is not real
it is an image,
but an image is not real.

If we seek God,
we must know what God is,
or how would we seek Him?

But we seek him through
what we know,
what we are told,
what we have read,
what we have created.
The product of our mind.

To find God,
the mind must be still,
not thinking about what is known,
that will not be God.

When the mind is still,
the thinker stops:
no belief,
no thought,
no language,
no knowledge,
no experience,
no dogmas,
no theories,
no image,
all of these bring restlessness.

Only no mind can be free,
when there is stillness.
The unknown becomes known.
The mind is free.

And love is revealed.

Mon Dieu!

I went to Japan
to find my God.
I found him in a church in Nagasaki.

I went to Uganda
to find my God.
I found him in Lango Cathedral.

I went to Honduras
to find my God.
I found him in Christians in La Ceiba.

But I couldn't understand the Word.

If I have the God, I was taught,
is there a better God in another language?

God Is Love

"Define God," the Bishop[10] said to the journalist,
"and I will answer your question."
The question in question being,
"Bishop, do you believe in God or not?"
Why should that be such a difficult question for a bishop?
Even for a bishop who said the resurrection was
"More than a conjuring trick with bones."
The answer lies in the charge to the journalist:
"Define God," rather a hard task you might think
for a theologian, not a journalist.
Bishops, although maybe not theologians, stick together.
To the rescue, from across the pond, comes a friendly episcopal voice[11]
agreeing that it is untenable to take seriously
the traditional view of God
and Bible stories as historical fact.
Reminding us of ostrich popes resisting Copernicus
and facing the reality of the Earth not being the center of the Universe.
With sympathy for the frustrated journalist,
and leaving the complexities of language,
to those who enjoy such games—
theologians, journalists, and the like,
we take the neat and easy way out.
"God is love."
To which what I want to ask is,
"Define love."

---

10. "While the controversy around me was at its height, I soldiered on in faith. Now, in retirement, the question is: How did I ever come to believe in all this?" Bishop David Jenkins.

11. Bishop John Shelby Spong.

God's Good Creation[12]

God created the world,
and all that was within,
and it was good.

So what is it with wasps and termites,
rats and jellyfish,
and viruses,
especially viruses?

Clerical scientists,
trying to square the circle,
tell us viruses are a natural part of God's good Creation,
play a positive part in nature,
and can be used in a positive, "redemptive" way.
But, inconveniently,
have a side-effect of harming humans,
as a "tiny" percentage
cause human disease.

12. Based on an article by the chair of the Royal College of Psychiatrists, spirituality and psychiatry group in *Church Times*, March 2020.

Taking Leave of God[13]

How did they manage to lose God?
And now lead their lives in glorious unawareness of his presence,
having transformed him from a cosmic figure
to an expression of their human virtue?

Somehow, they have given God an internal existence,
rather than the external reality declared by preceding generations,
leaving the Ten Commandments to be forged in our hearts,
rather than carved in stone.

They have substituted the characteristics of divinity
for their own deficient humanity,
thinking their paltry attributes are in the same league
as the Almighty Creator.

"Creation" is their new favorite,
substituting the unbelievable for the observable reality of life,
which is everywhere, in us all,
the "ground of all being,"
which conveniently allows them to lose all talk of
heavenly father, critical parent, a jealous, judgmental, perfect, angry deity,
who knows it all,
and is "out there somewhere."
This makes them feel more intellectual than naïve believers.

They have taken leave of God
and have no belief in an objective metaphysical Supreme Being,
which mocks their intelligence and prevents them from taking spirituality
into their own hands,
where they can be responsible for their own devoutness.

---

13. "Man's last and highest parting occurs when, for God's sake, he takes leave of God," Meister Eckhart.

In light of the evidence, perhaps they are right?

At least, history shows that religion continues when gods die.

New Gods for Old

When the old God broke, we made a new one
to give us comfort when we were upset
and needed a friend.
We made it with a face,
which was an improvement on the last model
who we couldn't see clearly, if at all,
and felt very distant from us most of the time.
The old design was often vague when trying to communicate,
and we could never be sure what it was trying to say.
But now the message comes through crystal-clear
and leaves us in no doubt what it wants us to know.
Far from judging us and making us feel in error,
our new one accepts us for what we are and gives full praise
to our piddling enthusiasm.
Always available, it appears personally devoted to me alone.
It is far more entertaining than the last one,
none of that boring stuff about people lost in the desert years ago
but instead contemporary updates about what matters now,
with music.
Altogether a vastly superior model to the classic edition,
which we should have ditched a long time ago.
No idea why it has taken us so long.

However,
it is very odd that the new model also involved an apple at its launch.

Say One for Me, Vicar

"Say one for me, Vicar,"
he says in passing me in the street
because he finds a dog collar amusing,
or perhaps his wife is ill, and he thinks I have a hotline
and will be more effective in getting through
to someone he doesn't think exists—
and is unlikely to make her better anyway—
but hedging his bets seems a good idea
in the circumstances.

"How's the Big Man upstairs today, Vicar?"
is another of their favorites,
as if I should know
and they are somehow excluded
from a knowledge of the Divine
because I am somehow superior to lay humanity
because a man put his hands on my head,
and have access to that all-important hotline
to that larger than life male in the skies.

"Nice day, your Reverence,"
is not a term of endearment, even if it sounds like it—
more a case of sneering ridicule,
which is partly our fault for doing a job where our title
demands we must be "respected,"
but it could be worse if we were an "Eminence,"
although a simple "Jack" would be nice.

"Going to your God-botherers club?"
is what we hear when things are turning nasty, and they are trying to be
offensive,
as if scorn and derision somehow distance them from what we stand for.

"*There's NoOneUpThere, you know,*" is their parting shot,
just in case we think there is.

It must be in their DNA
to only think of God this way,
or maybe have we taught them that which now so annoys us,
along with all the other fossilized beliefs we have insisted on?

Traits of God

My school is better than your school, Ofsted said so.
My angry indignation politics are superior to yours.
My religion is my God's own, my terrorism proves it.
My football team is better than yours, I can shout louder.
My Brexit views are right, you're simply wrong.
My war is a just one, you are just hostile.

Your God may be a loving Father showing mercy.
My God is judgmental, vindictive, and strict.

God's Word

"In the beginning was the Word, and the Word was with God, and
the Word was God."

—*John 1:1*.

The word can never be the thing.

A tree is a tree.
The word "tree" is not a tree.
A tree has its own life.
A tree is created in our image of a tree,
and only has meaning according to our experience of a tree;
good, if we painted its beauty,
bad, if we fell out of it in pain.
Our experience will determine what we think of a tree,
conditioned by where we live in the world
and what trees grow there,
and what we were taught about trees.
Its essential essence is not in the word,
which is only a concept from our past.
There is a colossal difference between a tree and the word.

God is God.
The word "God" is not God.

When we use the word "God," our mind is contaminated.
Tainted by past experiences,
poisoned by previous teachings,
obliterated by the opinions of others,
shattered by society,
tarnished by terror,
sullied by study,

blemished by not being our own,
ruined by being second hand.
The word has eliminated God.

Only a mind free of contamination of the word,
can encounter God.
Only a mind that is still and quiet,
calm, at peace and tranquil
can find communion with God.
A silent mind,
alone, innocent, empty and pure
can encounter God.
Intimacy without words.
Only a contemplative mind can achieve this.
The way is meditation.

Jesus is not the Word.
Jesus is the Logos.

Blaise Pascal

It is amazing to behold
that just using his brain,
Pascal discovered God
without a lot of pain.

He proved Christ's miracles
indisputably happened,
with a lifelong conviction
that never slackened.

The dude believed in Original Sin
and the need for Divine Grace,
to achieve eternal Salvation,
we all could embrace.

He argued against Free Will
and for Predestination,
doing so effectively
with much articulation.

This bozo tells us to believe in God,
just in case He exists.
If we don't, when we die,
we will look moronically foolish.
His questionable views
and religious position,
preclude him from the ranks
of 'progressive' Christian.

And make him a very bad Humanist.
Perhaps he was less confused with Mathematics?

No Fear in Love[14]

While the nations reached out to do My job,
serving communities,
caring for the poor and lonely,
feeding the hungry,
tending the sick,
what did you do with my house
in their time of need and fear?

You locked the doors,
and kept them out!
Denied them
a place of sanctuary and refuge,
and retreated into a safe, for you, virtual world,
hoping I would intervene and sort it out.

How can I ever show my face again
after you told them, "perfect love casts out fear."[15]

14. 1 John 4.7–17.
15. 1 John 4.18.

Hell's Bells

War is Hell.
Sartre thinks Hell is other people.
I know marriages which are sheer Hell.
Life can be Hell.
A mind can sink into Hell.
Human hatred is Hell.
Such Hells are real,
not invented by Christian theology
to reveal our fate if we get it wrong.

They say to make Holy Water,
you have to boil the Hell out of it.
Perhaps Hell has become a bit of a joke.

2020 rings out like Hell.
We are not out of it,
and it's not a joke.

Love Behind Legend[16]

Chance or originality played no part
when thoughts
of the divine conception of Jesus,
began in 9 AD.

Horus, a god of Egypt, born of the virgin Isis, around 1550 BC,
coincidentally received gifts from three kings when he was an infant.
Buddha, born about 600 BC, of the virgin Maya,
was also visited by the Holy Ghost.
Quirrnus, a Roman savior, born of a virgin in 6 BC,
whose death, another coincidence, bought complete darkness.
Indra, born of a virgin in Tibet in 8 BC, happened to ascend into heaven.
Adonis, a god of Babylon, born of a virgin mother Ishtar,
was later hailed as the queen of heaven,
like Mary.
So, nothing unique, after all.

But the father must not miss the chance of a Divine contribution either.
Perseus and Romulus were Divinely fathered,
as Greek and Roman myth tell us.
Not to be left out, the Egyptian pharaohs,
Alexander the Great, Caesar, and even Plato,
were reported to have Divine origins.

The early Christians would know all this.
By 10 AD the stories became the words of Matthew and Luke,
writing to affirm Christ's primary significance
with stories of wonder and amazement
to convince a listening multitude.

16. Based on John Shelby Spong, *Born of a Woman*.

Miraculous births were common in that other Testament,
unfamiliar to many modern Christians.
Ishmael, Isaac, Samson and Samuel
all followed the same pattern known to us elsewhere.
First, the angel appears to a frightened recipient,
who then receives a Divine message,
which is how all special births indicate a saving destiny.

It didn't happen, of course,
to think so misses the point.
Matthew and Luke don't do facts,
they do something far more important.
They save us from literalism
and in doing so provide a priceless wonder,
secret treasures, beauty,
mystery, awe, adoration
and the start of love.

Misogyny

They appeared to have forgotten
all about the virgin birth,
when the time came
for Mary to be "cleansed."

Purification was for a natural birth
but we are told that of Jesus
was far from natural,
Supernatural, in fact.
So why the need for cleansing?

A flimsy idea then,
this yarn about a Virgin birth,
that had to wait 200 years before
theologians made it "official."

No feminist movement in those times
to protect women from a
biblically imposed "cleansing,"
after a perfectly natural event,
caused, after all, by men's desire.

And now, for thirty-three days,
until blood is purified,
women can't touch holy things,
nor go to church,
such was their impurity.

"Unclean, unclean, hide those dirty mothers,"
would have been the cry
when women's value was rock bottom,
and misogyny ruled.

Virgin Birth

Not to have a dad is very sad,
unless you are a mixture of human and the Divine,
and mom can be all you need.
But scholars don't buy this fiction any more than we do.

I don't want a supernatural alien for my hero
and neither did St. Paul,
who assumed a fully human hero,
in his Christ.

Mark neither,
dismissing Divine intervention.
So, Matthew and Luke seem oddly at odds
with the rest of us,
and they certainly weren't eyewitnesses!
Maybe they had a secret agenda
to persuade doubting Thomas's?

Sixty-five years after the event,
Christian fireside chat came up with the idea:
To make the baby special was their hope
and thirty-five years later someone wrote it down,
for us to believe.

You don't come much more special
than being made to have been born of a virgin,
"the son of Mary,"
that's very special indeed.

Unless your paternity is unknown,
and a supernatural birth story
suggests incest and prostitution,

maybe illegitimacy,
are in your history,
which doesn't prevent you
having a holy origin and a holy life.

Because God can do that,
and show himself to the world.

For Our Sins

Time passes.
Jesus is born,
miraculously by a mother
who manages to avoid the contamination of sex.
Jesus dies.
He dies *"for our sins."*
Jesus, the rescuer, has arrived.
Augustine strikes again.
Someone has to pay the price
of Adam and Eve's sexual dalliance
and humankind's corruption.
Three cheers for the literal virgin birth
which saved Jesus from the sin of the fall.
Christians had turned their God into a child abuser,
prepared to sacrifice his only son on a cross.
Not a holy act at all in today's world.

PART III

Nativity and Christmas

Carol No. 6

"He came down to Earth,"
we sing this season,
reminding us of his descent:

"Suddenly, the Lord, descending."
"Love came down at Christmas."
"Born for us on earth below."
"Down to such a world as this!"
"The Angel of the Lord came down."
"And all the bells on Earth shall ring."
"So God imparts to human hearts."
"O Holy Child of Bethlehem,
descend to us, we pray."
"'He came down to earth from Heaven."

From Heaven, He came down,
reminding us of his original abode.

"In Heaven, the bells are ringing."
"Him whom Heaven and Earth adore."
"He hath opened the heavenly door."
"Thus, to come from highest bliss."
"The heavenly babe you there shall find."
"And all the angels in Heaven shall sing."
"Hail, the heaven-born Prince of Peace."
"The blessings of his Heaven."
"Fit us for Heaven to live with thee there."
"Is our Lord in heaven above."
"He came down to Earth from Heaven."

He came down to Earth from Heaven.
"Veiled in the flesh, the Godhead see."

Down to a meaningless worldview,
except for church leaders,
fearful for their authority.
Living on the flat earth
with Heaven above and Hell below,
scared to admit the Earth was not
the center of the Universe,
and maybe God has interests elsewhere?

"Veiled in flesh" is a troublesome image,[17]
for the divine rescuer to fulfill,
or the believer to comprehend.

Like unwrapping the bandages around the Invisible Man
to expose the body temporarily revealed.
"Here I am, over here, in a stable."
Bindings to be re-round when invisibility calls again,
at Ascension.

---

17. "A divine substance being plunged in flesh and coated with it like chocolate or silver plating," John Robinson, *Honest to God.*

Nativity: "Then Don't Believe It" — I

"Now the birth of Jesus the Messiah took place in this way."

—*Matthew 1*

"I can't come to your church, Vicar," he said.

"Why on earth not?" Vicar replied.

"I don't believe it," he said.

"Don't believe what?" Vicar asked.

"Virgins having babies," he said.

"Then don't believe it," said Vicar.

Midnight Mass

Silence.

Bells rest, the dust settles, and the bats return.
People are still thoughtful, praying.
All is quiet,
all is peaceful.
Even the priest resists his trademark flow of words and words and words.
Nothing moves to spoil the magical, mystical silence
of a country church at midnight
on Christmas Eve.

Snow lies softly, and fresh white flakes float down from on high,
bringing the flesh of Christ
from that heavenly place, so cold,
yet flesh arrives warm on the baby in the straw,
as God reveals himself at last
to a searching world,
so we are told.

And church folk sing of crowded skies where angels
announce this impossible coming
and their knees hurt from too long kneeling,
to greet the child who no one yet knows is born
and who starts Christmas fun.

To ask the questions, the older children are desperate to ask
would spoil the atmosphere,
and pop their festive balloons
and make you a party-pooper.
Where does he come from if he comes down?
How do you make flesh from God?
What are angels, and can we really hear them sing?

And why wait?
Why so long if humankind needs this message, as they all say?

Best just take it as real,
as the priest so movingly preaches,
and the grown-ups tell us really happened,
and the truth melts slowly away like the snow,
leaving the real grass beneath to recover
after its seasonal dressing as a magic wonderland
with Father Christmas and his elves;
and folk can return to their common sense
when the midnight magic wears off
and the children grow not to question it either.

Easier to let the man behind the myth melt slowly away
and save us the effort of taking his teaching seriously,
when the New Year begins.

"Then Don't Believe It"—II

"But I don't believe the other stuff either," he said.

"What other stuff?" asked Vicar.

"Angels bringing news of positive pregnancy tests."

"Then don't believe it," said Vicar.

Three Gifts from Three Kings

It must have been an expensive stable
to take all that *kingly gold,*
to pay for what must have been
less than five-star facilities.
Somebody made a killing that night.
He must have seen them coming,
before leaving them to face a life of poverty.
Must have been some left though,
a hundred-mile flight to Egypt would have been costly.
Maybe they had to sell some of the other gifts as well?

Mary's fumigation with the perfume of *godly frankincense*
smoking through the stable
reminds us of Mesopotamia or Ancient China.
No premonition of
today's aromatherapy industry, though.
Which is a pity.
Mary could have made her fortune.
If businesswomen were allowed
by the men of first-century Palestine.

Myrrh would also come in handy
with a newborn baby—
a carminative herb,
which also helps the pain of teething.
At least Mary and Joseph would get some sleep.
Best not think about anointing to prepare for *sacrifice.*
That would spoil Christmas.

No wonder we have to summarize the whole thing and sing:
"*King and God and sacrifice.*"

Gold, Frankincense, and Myrrh,
the three traditional gifts to kings and the gods.

But why the intrigue?
Magi? Wise Men? Kings?
Sorcerers? Astrologers?
Why the confusion?
Who would bring a newborn baby,
gold and frankincense and myrrh?
Who came "from the East,"
which could be from a dozen different countries?
Following a star,
which don't really stop in the sky to mark a birth,
especially of an unknown child?
Were mystic magicians present at the birth of God,
or does this narrative mean something else entirely?

Maybe we are just at a school Christmas pageant,
unquestioning, but happy in our cluelessness?

"Then Don't Believe It" — III

"Nor the next bit," he said.

"What next bit?" asked Vicar.

"Nearly due pregnant mum traveling a hundred miles on a donkey,
and a dad who didn't book ahead. Hotels all full.
Stuck outside in a stable. Filthy animals. Mucky straw.
Who wrote that stuff anyway? Must have been a man.
At least it wasn't snowing."

"Then don't believe it," said Vicar.

What's in a Name?

The Queen of Sheba got the gift idea first though
on her visit to King Solomon,
with her camel train and great quantities of gold.
And before her, at the temple in Miletus,
King Seleucus II Callinicus Pogon, of that heroic name,
made the same offerings to Apollo,
beating the Magi to it by more than 200 years.

Representing the three ages of man,
seven hundred years later, the church names them.
Balthazar, the twenty-year-old Ethiopian
unpacks the gift of myrrh.

Middle-aged Arabian Melchoir fares better,
with the frankincense,
a symbol of prayer is a better option than implying death.

Or maybe old Caspar, sixty years, out of Tarsus,
gave the frankincense, not, as recorded, the gold?
I hope it was the gold,
a symbol of virtue beats the others
when pleasing proud parents.

Which tradition to favor?
It makes a lot of difference to the story.
No one is even certain who these generous gift-givers were.
Wise men, magi, astronomers, astrologers,
court advisors, scientists, magicians even.

Choose your tradition wisely before you decide.
I like that of the Eastern church, which gives us a glorious twelve Magi.
I wonder what the other nine gifts could have been?

Socks, aftershave, cuddly toy, chocolate maybe?
The Syriacs certainly knew how to party.

Our avaricious children of today
would be mightily unimpressed,
if they only found three presents under the tree!
They might like the gold, though.
And believe it all,
because we now know who they were.

Or do we?

"Then Don't Believe It"—IV

"Nor the next bit," he said.
"What next bit?" asked Vicar.
"The Bethlehem bit. What's that all about?
Jesus was a child in Nazareth.
Why drag them all the way to Bethlehem
just because Micah said a messiah would be born there?
'Jesus of Nazareth,' Vicar, remember?"

"Then don't believe it," said Vicar.

The Crib

St. Francis had a good idea in the Assisi of the twelfth century
when he had a thought which would leave its mark on history.

Making a live crib scene in a cave wouldn't take much energy,
but it would tell of the birth of the baby Jesus with his family.

Francis bought into the cave all the animals from the stable,
their imaginations to inspire, with a genuine baby in a cradle.

To leave the people a memory for the future, the saint undertook,
before they could read it for themselves, much later, in the Book.

So originated the tradition of devotions at the Christmas Crib,
which achieved his original mission and encouraged worship.

Now the clergy make a big event of bringing out the baby Jesus
on Christmas Eve,
making it a special fun time for all those present to enjoy what they believe.

But nobody is thinking of the babies dying around the world,
through poverty, through religion, through the human species inhumanity
to itself.

And so the whole point of Christmas drifts silently past us again.
And love gets lost.

"Then Don't Believe It" — V

"Nor those shepherds," said the man.

"Oh, the shepherds," said Vicar.

"Yes, those shepherds," said the man.

"Sudden daylight in the middle of the night and that angel, with more news, and with his mates this time, singing.

Would you let smelly, filthy, dirty, sheep and shepherds into a maternity ward?

Give me a break. Really?" said the man.

"Then don't believe it," said Vicar.

Presence

What do you buy someone who has everything?

The royal family spend a tenner each,
on gifts of fun but no value.
Benefit moms max out their cards
with no thought of future payments,
not to disappoint little Maisie and Wayne.
Brainwashed from adverts,
constantly stimulating the pleasure cortex,
we unconsciously buy all we need,
promised to "have the best Christmas ever."

Wrapping paper, tinsel tied
with bows and ribbons and tag,
enclose the gift preciously sourced.
Ripped open in seconds to add to the pile
on the floor,
and another offering carefully placed aside
to be returned to the store,
if it falls short.

Much thought was given to loved one's choice,
unless purchased at last minute
in a department store on the way back from
lovers nest.

In the turmoil of festive madness
no one stops to think about what is needed,
rather than wanted.
What would make a difference rather,
than be forgotten,
as soon as the sales open?

How to convert the mystery of the season
into a life-changing miracle.

Yet we sing it all the time now,
a clue which passes us by,
as the world rolls into another year of pain
of money, success, status.

"Yet what I can I give him. Give my heart."

The gift of Divine love gets discarded,
as easily as the tie and perfume.
Too much effort to maintain,
even for a day as family rifts appear.
Much easier to buy a present,
and ignore the Christ child's presence
in the coming year.

"Then Don't Believe It" — VI

"And what about that star?" said the man.
"What about the star?" said Vicar. "They do exist, you know."
"Don't get me going on the star Vicar.
What, a star, circling the universe, destination earth
stopping in the sky to shine on a stable
just to illuminate the birth of a child who no one knows.
Not in my world, Vicar," said the man.
"Then don't believe it," said Vicar.

"Oh, Christmas Tree"

The tree people of the psalms
olive, palm, and cedar,
celebratory symbols to worship God,
flourish and do good.
Whereas the wicked are blown in the wind
and fade away.

We have moved a long way from myrtle trees
and cypress for idolatrous celebration,
since Isaiah united them in the worship of God.

Like Christmas itself, the pagan evergreen
is converted to be made worthy,
and Boniface's ax sparks an idea.

Now confused Christians erect their tree
in the dark, depths of winter
to welcome the light of the world,
as if it is a Christian thing to do.
And confused churches follow suit
not to miss out on a good thing,
adding pagan holly and ivy for good measure.

Sitting rooms are illuminated
with twinkly colors,
and glass baubles and polar bears state
the names of grandchildren and loved Uncle Tom.
While flashing LEDs, like icicles, surround the house,
shining out their pretend Christian message,
as the wicked scurry by in the dark.

So Christ sits above the triangular trinity tree
like the treetop fairy,
despairing the plastic branches
devoid of meaning,
looking down on his Christmas people.

And wonders
if they will ever see the light.

"Then Don't Believe It"—VII

"And how do three kings get in on the act?" asked the man.

"Wise men, you mean?" said Vicar.

"Have you seen a Christmas card lately, Vicar?" asked the man.

"Three kings on camels,

trekking across the hills, day and night,

only for the magic star to get them lost in Jerusalem.

'Find the king,' cries Herod, sending them off to search.

Why search? What's happened to the magic guiding star?

And led, do you get this, led—by a star! To Bethlehem, where it stopped!

Stopped, Vicar! Stopped in the sky. Brian Cox will be apoplectic.

Where they give a brand-new baby gold and perfume and herbs. What!

And if the baby grew up poor, Vicar, what happened to the gold, eh?

Tell me that?

Really Vicar, too much communion wine?"

"Then don't believe it," said Vicar.

Starstruck

A star floating in space announces the birth of a king,
a magical star floating slowly across the skies.
But it does sound familiar, this floating star.
Abraham, Isaac, and Moses
all had their births announced by a star.

Heaven up, Earth down, Hell below,
a dead worldview.
Floating stars don't appear in today's worldview.
The beauty of stars is in galaxies and the Milky Way,
Andromeda, Alpha Centauri,
not in announcing an earthly event.

In the real world, no floating star leads the magi.
Floating stars are more myth and magic in which to wrap the baby Jesus,
to help hide him amongst the tinsel and fairy lights.

Until he can be seen no longer,
behind the dazzling lights of Christmas.

"Then Don't Believe It"—VIII

"And then, Vicar, it all goes pear-shaped," said the man.

"How?" asked Vicar?

"Well, NoOneUpThere, you call God, gave the kings a dream to push off home without telling their new King mate about the baby as he wants to kill it.

So mom, dad, and brand-new baby jump on the donkey again and run for it, to Egypt of all places.

While get this, Vicar, their kingly mate goes and slaughters all the local new born boys.

Not very Christmassy, Vicar, you must agree?"

"Then don't believe it," said Vicar.

Operation Rescue Christmas

The celebrity-struck, money-mad,
gift-greedy, consumer society
we have created,
only makes contact with Christianity,
at Christmas.

Perhaps we need to demystify the story,
cease the fictionalized illusion,
and rescue its truth, so they can believe.

Rather than letting them think
Progressive Christians just want to shatter their illusion,
and destroy their festival
by telling them, the Nativity is a story,
and not real.

"Then Don't Believe It"—IX

"I don't need telling, Vicar.

I don't believe a word of it.

It's not real. It can't happen. It didn't happen. No one believes it."

"Then don't believe it," said Vicar,

thinking of her congregation who believe every word.

"If it stops you from seeing the baby as one of us, you shouldn't believe it.

If it gets in the way of the real Jesus, you shouldn't believe it.

If this story sounds like a fairy-tale and banishes the baby to an unreal world of fairy lights, then ditch it."

Natalis Solis-invicti

Snow and robins on the cards,
it must have been winter when they kept the baby warm
in straw and swaddling cloths.
But sheep are kept indoors during cold winter nights,
likewise, their herders, not out watching their flocks.
Obviously, Luke didn't know any shepherds.

How do you forget God's birthday?
Why didn't somebody make a note,
of the birthday of Jesus?
Strange, no record of birthday cards or parties
for one so famous from his birth.

Come December 17, and the Romans roll out their
festival to honor Saturn, god of agriculture,
and mark the new solar cycle
with merrymaking and exchange of family gifts.
Their Mithraism worship of the Persian
"God of Light"
was popular with the Roman army.

Time passes,
three hundred and thirty-six years,
and now the Romans celebrate their sun god,
Natalis Solis-invicti, "the birthday of the unconquered sun,"
their winter solstice,
and record the date in their almanac: twenty-fifth December.

Constantine converts to Christianity
and early church leaders steal a pagan holiday,
which celebrates the rebirth of the sun,
and turn it into a festival celebrating the birth of Jesus,
God, the Son.

"Then Don't Believe It" — X

"Listen, Vicar. I gotta break it to you . . . I'm post-Christian . . .
I don't believe it anymore. I don't believe any of it." Said the man.

"I understand." said the Vicar. "Lots of people think the same today after.
After a childhood of being told it's all true by the church, they grow up,
think it through and don't believe it anymore.
You are not alone."

Christmas Past, Christmas Present— an Old Testament Christmas Story[18]

Easily forgotten, ignored, not even read
the Old Testament provides the clue,
to the greatest story ever told:

The story of the Nativity of Jesus.

As scholars insist,
to understand the Jesus story
first, to understand the Old Testament is essential,
even though we hear the cry,
"What's that got to do with it?"

In this story,
the familiar and favorite characters from the school nativity play
slowly unfold from the pages of the Old Testament.

Adam and Eve in the Garden of Eden,
God revealed as the Creator.

The grey-bearded prophets,
Abraham, Micah, Isaiah provide the prophecies.

Joseph and his colorful coat,
where dreams originate.

Moses and the very first census,
and precedes that of Quirinius.

Angels,
borrowed from the Temple at Jerusalem.

18. Based on my school nativity play, 2006.

Manoah's wife told she will bear a son,
three thousand years before Gabriel visits Mary.

The Psalms of David,
tell their story.

Jeremiah's shepherds look after his flock,
as did the terrified ones in the fields at night.

The Queen of Sheba visits the wise King Solomon,
five hundred years before Jesus.

The Kings of Tarshish and Sheba visit and King Seba brings gold,
as did the three wise men.

The wicked Pharaoh searches for a boy to kill,
like Herod after the Innocents.

They are all here,
and all appear in the Old Testament Christmas story.

The origins of the angels, dreams, the star,
Bethlehem, the birth to a virgin, the shepherds,
and the wise men with their gold and frankincense and myrrh
all reveal their hidden origins in the stories of the Old Testament.

So arrives *"Christmas Past, Christmas Present,"*
revealing how the old stories and characters
from the past,
have been used in the Christmas story
to tell us something important
about Jesus in today's world.

Early Christian writers wanted to say something
special about the baby Jesus,

and his growing into an adult who became Our Lord.
They took characters and signs
familiar to the people of their day,
and wove them into a new story about Jesus.

They were trying to impress on the people
the significance of the baby in the crib.
New life sprang from familiar stories
and so the tale was told,
as we know and love it.

An Old Testament story became our New Testament nativity.

"Then Do Believe It"

"But if you see in this unbelievable Christmas story
the man who grew up to show us the meaning of life,
to reveal the heart of the universe
and to help us handle the most powerful thing in the world,
love,
Then do believe it," said Vicar.

"By the way, do you know the Easter story?
Now there's something for you really not to believe!"

Peace on Earth, Goodwill to All Men

It all starts so well,
Mother's unconditional love
safe, secure, happy
mutual togetherness:
the true blueprint for living,
where harmony rules.
Our original state of innocence.

Then it all starts to go wrong.
Life gets in the way.
We start to be taught to hate,
by those who claim to love us.

My friend or partner who just sees things differently
is now the enemy,
foe, not friend.
Divorce soars.
Relationships fail.
Communication falters.
Children suffer over love lost.
Narcissism grows.

We don't do religion
or pray or meditate or slow down,
so no chance
of hearing that still small voice of calm
over the clamor,
where Jesus is crowded out
with his message of
tolerance, forgiveness, care, compassion, acceptance, non-judgment,
equality, peace, patience, kindness, truth, hope, joy, self-control.
And love.

We threw him out with the bathwater of rejected Christian myth,
with virgin births and Father Christmas,
failing to see the message behind the man

Peace on Earth.
Goodwill to all men, with exceptions

God in a Manger

What a terrible and unnecessary journey
for a pregnant girl bearing her illegitimate child,
to travel a hundred miles on a donkey
with no overnight stops for a virgin defiled.

No census had called them to Bethlehem,
from Nazareth, they had to be sent,
to fulfill the prophet, Micah
was the gospel writer's intent.

A warm stable to shelter from the snow,
would have been nice for the miracle child,
also a manger, with holly and ivy,
plus a robin to gaze at the baby mild.

The shepherds were not easily scared
and stayed firmly in fields with their flock,
the idea of visiting a baby
would have been a terrible shock.

Wise men by definition have wisdom
so, no journey into the unknown,
they know stars don't stop in the sky,
to magi, a fact well known.

Nor shine down to an unnamed house,
to bestow gifts and valuable presents,
gold, frankincense, and myrrh
are too good to waste on these lowly peasants.

To end with an irate king
who murdered children, all-male,

because he was jealous and angry
makes an incredible tale.

And now we have angels singing,
a heavenly note in the skies,
but on closer inspection you see,
a clue, a myth this story implies.

None of this really happened,
this tale is daft from the start,
but God, in this stable story
touches many a heart,
and the baby God in a manger
engages us year after year,
which is why the grown-up Jesus
helps us live without any fear.

"Then Do Believe It, Because . . ."

The season of myths and legends,
which we call Christmas-tide,
is fraught with activity
chiefly the school nativity,
which makes mothers preoccupied
with countless tasks of making things,
for which they have an ability
but maybe not qualified,
like costumes for tiny kings
and delicate angel wings
viewed by infants satisfied
that Miss will be pleased
when costumes get scrutinized.

Parents and most adults,
remain confused from their own school days,
which have passed them by in a haze,
and results in them still believing the story,
as if it is mandatory.
When they rarely stop to consider
it seems implausible,
and far from sensible,
but unable to sort facts from fantasies,
they can't see the fallacies involved
so take Christmas traditions on board,
as if they are eternal,
failing to realize
that medieval ceremonial
celebrating the pagan winter solstice,
should make them recognize
the contemporary carnival,
we call Christmas.

Using holly, ivy, and mistletoe
started in the winter solstice,
where snowmen scared evil winter spirits,
when the weather was freezing,
with no medieval Yule log to
warm the chilly evenings.
Christmas trees were heathen hangings
at Saturnalia, for the Roman legion.
Carols were winter solstice songs,
sung in every region,
full of idolatrous slogans,
and candles a solstice sign of spring
full of new year omens.

A fourth-century bishop, Nicholas by name,
gives us our Father Christmas.
But still no date for the birth of Jesus.

No matter.
The date is not important.
If we didn't have this story
to tell of Gods glory,
we would have to make it up.
The greatest story ever told,
of angels and gifts of gold.
A story of hidden meaning
secretly pleading,
that man might at last see
where this tale is leading.

God on earth.
Love in action.

A presence to give away,
whatever your religion.

PART IV

Jesus, Miracles, and Crucifixion

Roots or Wings

"Christian atheists,"
is the name Richard Dawkins gives to those who
believe in the message of Jesus,
but don't want to make him into a magic man
coming down from Heaven,
walking on water
and coming alive again.

They have disposed of theism,
rejecting any Supreme Being
and replaced it with humanism,
believing in reason and common humanity
where science rules the Universe,
and is not subverted by fundamentalist zealots
or supernatural beliefs.

With no need of knowledge from any god
or holy books
to teach moral values.
Where there is no hereafter
only now,
to be lived with joy.
Where humans are free
to give meaning and shape to their lives
through thought and experience.
To make a humane society
with acceptance and tolerance
and kindness and love,
inclusive
not judging or condemning or excluding
like the church of Jesus has become,

if you don't toe the line and follow the rules
of who and how to love.

Roman Marcus Tullius Cicero was keen on humanity
believing in active virtue and human dignity,
benevolence, compassion, and mercy.
And Rabelais' hero saves the monastery,
while useless monks chant meaningless Latin
in their religious sanctuary,
and the real world passes them by.

Maybe Jesus would have liked humanism,
if they hadn't made him God.

Now You See Him, Now You Don't

Some say, Jesus didn't exist, some say,
that's one way of solving the problem.
It was, after all, a popular name.
Nothing in Roman records of the time. Fact.
"No independent evidence of the man, my Lord," says the prosecution
at the Christ Myth Theory trial.

Now you see him. Now you don't.

All a figment of the church's imagination then,
allegories that started to be believed as fact,
about this secret figure.

Early Jewish tradition calls him a magician.
They are in good company with those who think you can't walk on water.
Or feed 5000 with two fish and a loaf.
At least they believed he existed
but as a Jewish preacher.
No claim to be God.
No intent to found a religion.

Facts:
Baptized by John the Baptist.
Called "disciples."
Public disorder at the temple.
Crucified by Romans near Jerusalem.
A Galilean.
Workplace confined to Galilee and Judea.
Disciples continued after his death,
some despite persecution.

I suppose being remembered 2000 years later for eight things isn't too bad?
Better than most of us will achieve.
Now you see him. Now you don't.

Facts, not fantasies.
History, not histrionics.
Science, not superstition.
Don't tell the man in the pew.
Don't scare the horses.
Don't upset the children.

Now they see him. Now they don't

The Remarkable Magdalene—*John* 20

On the first day, still dark, she came to the tomb.
Stone gone.
She told them *"They have taken the Lord out of the tomb, and we do not know where they have laid him."*
The Lord has been taken. The Lord.
The. The. The. Our.
So she cries. Weeping. Outside the tomb.

She looked inside. Two angels. In white. *"Why do you cry?"* they ask.
"They have taken away my Lord, and I do not know where they have laid him."
Taken away, my Lord. My Lord.
My. My. My. Mine.

Jesus asks, *"Why are you weeping?"*
She turns. Someone to help her quest. The gardener.
"Sir, if you have carried him away, tell me where you have laid him, and I will take him away."
I will take him away.
But . . . claiming his body.
Odd that.
Only mothers and wives can do that. In first-century Judea.
No sign of the virgin Mary asking for the body, though.
"What can it mean, this claiming His body?"

"Mary!"
"Rabbouni!"

The remarkable Magdalene.
Leader of women.
Carer of disciples.
Cleansed of demons.
Key position in the Jesus movement.

Chief mourner at the tomb.

Sharer of the resurrection.

Announcer of the Ascension.

Identified by later Popes as a woman taken in adultery.

As women of the street who washed Jesus's feet with her tears.

Trashed by the church. Cast as a prostitute with no shred of evidence.

Patriarchal attempts to suppress her flesh-and-blood presence in Jesus's life.

Only witness of the unascended Jesus.

"Do not hold me, for I have not yet ascended to the Father," He says.

Was she was going to hold him?

Why wouldn't she hold him?

Mothers and wives do that.

In first-century Judea.

"They have taken away my Lord."

Wife of Jesus,

mother of his children,

God willing.

The Jesus Fish

Iesous Christos, Theou Yios, Soter

Persecuted by the Romans
for not worshipping their gods,
the fish appears,
on tombs and meeting places
to show friend from foe.

Words within a word.
A sacred sign,
for secret believers.

Not such a strange sign
for fishers of men,
and Gospel stories
and grilled fish after rising.

I, Iota, Iesous, Jesus.
Ch, Chi, Christos, anointed.
Th, Theta, Theou, God.
Y, Upsilon, Yios, Son.
S, Sigma, Soter, Savior.

The sign of the fish,
the twofold nature of Jesus:
True man and True God,
the Holy Trinity.

Jesus Christ, Son of God, (our) Savior

Someone Else's Poem

Who will love a displaced person, a transvestite, a downtrodden wife,
whose voice is voiceless and goes unheard?
"Not me," said the politician, the bishop, the husband!
"The power is mine and mine it shall be,
I won't reach out to equality,
and my ivory tower will protect me."

Who will love an unknown
and share with them the glow of fame?
"Not me," said the celebrity, the star of the show,
the TV presenter who everyone knows,
"It would diminish my own sense of ego and worth,
my status depends on being above most.
My low self-esteem would be exposed at last."

Who will take pity on the poor,
and feed the crowd around the door?
"Not me," said the banker, behind his high gates,
"I do what I can in all honesty,
but to give it away is beyond me.
There could be a crash, and then what would I do?
A million doesn't go far, you know."

Who will love and love and love some more,
ask naught in return, and keep no score?
"I will," says the Christ, "and if they kill me,
the love will remain through eternity
for all I've created returns unto me."

"From dust were ye made and dust ye shall be."

Anarchy

Our young people
with best intentions
to save the planet,
the ice cap,
the polar bears,
use protests and placards
and strident voices.

While their protest is hijacked
by brutish anarchists,
closing streets,
while innocent people
can't get to work,
for the only sin
of disagreeing
with the views of the mob.

A little thoughtless,
some kinder souls would observe,
reminding naïve activists
that Jesus didn't have much to say
about polar bears,
but quite a lot about
how to treat your neighbor,
to pray for those who persecute you,
and even love your enemy.

His way is the way of love,
Not revolution.

Be Quiet

When Christ tells us to be calm
as the storms hit our lives,
He is in good company.

When the therapist tells the client
that the practice of mindfulness
will reduce his anxiety,
that is sound advice.

When people want to move
from the hubbub of the city
to the peace of a rural idyll,
their instinct is sound.

When Pascal observes:
"All human misery comes from a single cause,
Mankind's inability to sit still in a quiet room, alone,"
He is so right.

Power to Save[19]

"Who then is this, that even the wind and the sea obey him?"
—*Mark 4*

Who indeed controls the perfect storm?
No man I know has this unnatural power to bring to my world an unworldly calm.
Creation may recall evil in the waters
and the chaos of the seas
and leviathan being thwarted by God.
But telling the storm to stop?
That doesn't happen.

But long ago,
revealed in Psalm,
God did these things
and those in ships saw wondrous things
the Lord did in the deep.
Commanding stormy winds
to lift the waves to heaven,
so men cried to him in distress
and he made the storm be still
and hushed the waves of the sea.

But Jesus sleeps,
the storm rages on,
so, men cried to him in distress
and he sleeps on.
Awake, awake, put on strength,
and do something.

---

19. "Peace, be still. Do not be afraid. I AM"'I AM' Gk. Ego eimi—have no fear,"
Mark 4:35–41; Psalms 89:8–10; 107:23–29.

Herein lies the meaning, not the myth.
Why the story tells us he did these things when he didn't.
Like stupid disciples then,
we reach the wrong conclusion
and think it happened.
No unnatural powers to calm storms
but to remind men that in past writings,
that a storm was a symbol.
A symbol of trials and tribulations,
disasters and woes,
saved by their God, who brought them through.

We are told this reminds them of Jesus,
who saves us as their God did them.
Myth but with a message.
Extraordinary power,
not supernatural,
but the power to save.
Power to calm the storms in our lives.
Calm through turmoil and chaos.
If we would wake him and call.
If we would hear his words.

Take Heart[20]

"He came toward them, walking on the lake."
—*Mark 6*

Couldn't he make up his mind?
Walking toward them one minute,
intending to pass by the next?

But it sounds familiar?
God reveals himself to his people
by *"passing by."*

Now we get it.
If that's what God did then,
we must make Jesus do it now.

If their God did wonderful things,
in Moses's time gone by,
so must Jesus, now.

Nothing much has changed in 2000 years.
We still don't see the real Jesus,
just the magic Jesus.

The magic of Jesus, the church wants us to see.
The magic of myth made to be real.
The magic man, walking on water.
About stories, they pretend are real.
So, in telling stories, they hide the real miracle,
the miracle of Christ in us now.

20. "Take heart, it is I; do not be afraid," Mark 6.

But buried under the myth and magic,
hiding the truth of Christ.
His gift of agape.

Wrong End of the Stick

"And he said, 'Go and say to this people: "Keep listening, but do not comprehend; keep looking, but do not understand."'"

—*Isaiah 6:9*

You can't blame the people.
It's not their fault they get it wrong.
Always missing the point.
Getting the wrong end of the stick.
Barking up the wrong tree.

We told them, so it's our fault.
Church and clergy and school.
Stories we pretended were real,
but hadn't the courage to correct
at the death of Father Christmas.

Old Testament stories not really suitable for the children,
too much sex, murder, and blood.
Best to stick with that nice Jesus,
he loved the little children.

So, let the OT gather dust
and take the easy option in the NT.
Stories we can believe in,
pretend are real,
because they happened.

We didn't tell them they were a literary construct,
with a hidden meaning.
That miracles have a 'Christological' purpose
to tell us something about the nature of Jesus,

not what he did.
That they are "eschatological" and lead us
to the fulfillment of the "end-time" with Jesus.
Words far too difficult for the average pew-person,
let alone the little children.

So, forget the inside miracle meanings,
the allusions not seen,
the significance not grasped,
the wonder not understood.
Blissful ignorance is easier than trying to remedy
the misinterpretations of a lifetime.

It's not their fault they get the wrong end of the stick after all.
One day they might even ask a question.
That would be nice.

Weddings and Wine

"On the third day, there was a wedding in Cana of Galilee,"
surely there is a hint there?

Heaven, the ultimate wedding feast,
when Christ and Church join.

Eschatology is such a big word!

A wedding, a symbol of God's kingdom,
not a party on Earth at all,
which makes Cana much less fun
with no drunken revels to anticipate,
but will there be wine?

New wine, the best wine, would be good,
replacing water with fine wine even better.
No new wine in old skins,
new skins, please.

One hundred and twenty gallons may sound good,
but such abundance can't be right,
far too much for even the thirstiest.
Another symbol maybe,
the overflowing joy of the Savior's Day.
But please don't preach that it just tells us
of God's bountifulness,
and miss the point of the narrative.

A believer's union through bread and wine
would truly be a miracle,
like those of Dionysius,
the god of wine,

or Philo exclaiming,
"The Word brings forth wine instead of water."

At Cana, the Word is real:
An overflowing banquet of bread and wine,
for all God's people.

Eucharist and eschatology are such big words.

Fast-food Numbers Game

Five. This Jewish number rings a bell
of loaves and Pentateuch books.
Feed the people of Tabgha, He said,
and 5000 Capernium Jews fed.

"Taking the five loaves,
he looked up to heaven, blessed and broke the loaves."

Leaving twelve baskets over.
This number also rings a bell,
twelve tribes of Israel,
can't be a coincidence, can it?

Four. A Gentile number this time,
a hint of Gentile empires and an Israel overrun.
Take seven loaves, another number hint.
Seventy Gentile nations.

"He took the seven loaves,
and after giving thanks, he broke them and gave them to his disciples."

Feed 4000, this time at Decapolis,
this meal was for the Greeks.
Leaving seven baskets over.
Then he said to them, "Do you not yet understand?"

"Feed" the Jews, then the Greeks
these miracles imply.
Not a shared picnic or magic
but the Gospel's aim:
Salvation for all,
Gentiles and Jews,

nourished by God's Word.
The Bread of Life.
The new Moses.

"While they were eating, he took a loaf of bread,
and after blessing it, he broke it, gave it to them, and said,
'Take; this is my body.'"

The Wisdom of God offered to humans,
in a banquet of bread and wine.
The Eucharistic meaning of the miracle.

Then he said to them, "Do you not yet understand?"
Two thousand years later, do we?

Ending

Crucified by Pilate,
as demanded by rebellious Jews,
an executed criminal
with others like him, on either side.

Not left to rot, like other Roman enemies,
no feeding of the crows on crucified slaves for him.

Buried with others in disgrace
unmarked, unknown,
far from the city.
A common grave
or a massed tomb,
not a special case worthy of special care.

Maybe a rich man saved him from this fate,
and reluctant Romans allowed Jewish burial customs,
recalling Joseph in Pharaoh's jail,
and placing Jesus in Joseph's tomb?
Both imprisoned heroes.
Or did they move him to a secret place?

Nevertheless,
dispatched,
humiliated,
mortified,
disgraced,
dishonored,
vilified,
defamed,
discredited,
scandalous,

a shameful death,
not laid to rest.

His friends fail to claim his body,
or find it in a tomb.
The women tried but failed.
His rising to Heaven would help them out.

So much myth, magic, and maybes
but, for Pilate, problem solved.

For us, not the end
but a new beginning.

Scapegoat

A blot on the Christian landscape,
rescuing the Romans and blaming the Jews
for Christ's death.

It was the Romans that did it.
What a tragedy.
Making the Jews the villains.

Pilate freed of innocent blood
by the washing of his hands
and pleading Christ's innocence three times.
Not me. Not guilty.
"I am innocent of this man's blood.
What evil has he done?"
What else do I have to say?
I'll invent a custom not seen before,
release a prisoner, Barabbas, *bar,* the son; *Abba,* God.
Release the son of God.
How clear do I need to be,
to be free of blame?

"Crucify him, crucify him," they cried.
"His blood be on us and our children."
Who wrote this death wish from the Jews, we ask?
Why, in sacred scripture, such as pain and suffering,
an excuse for anti-Semitism?
Now we Christians can be anti-Jew,
they killed our Jesus!
Not the Romans, not Pilate,
the Jews, the people of Judah,
they did it.
Damn them.

The Synoptic story reveals the setup.

On the Holy night of Passover, they arrested Jesus,
these Sanhedrin, these Jewish authorities,
that night of Passover, they arrested Jesus.
"Judas, one of the twelve, arrived;
with him was a large crowd with swords and clubs,
from the chief priests and the elders of the people."
Unlikely.
They were out celebrating,
not interested enough in a troublemaker
to leave the party.
They couldn't violate Torah law by judging at night,
not allowed. Must be daylight.
The Romans could cope till dawn.

But why, oh why, blame the Jews?

It was the Romans that did it.
Fact.
What a disgrace.
What a tragedy.
Making the Jews the villains,
just to build their church
and cause such suffering over the years.

Eternal Salvation

This veil of tears
full of earthly suffering
has to be patiently accepted,
borne in serene resignation
to His infinite wisdom,
then transformed as offering to God
to ensure eternal salvation
when the grim reaper has called.

Saving the soul from sin and its consequences
humankind's universal predicament,
God's plan for humanity's salvation
after the Fall of Adam.
As taught by the church and expected to be believed,
is one way of looking at it.

Eternal salvation goes with invalid Fall of Adam,
as there is no fall to recover from.
Simply eat, drink, and be merry
this is all you get.
Enjoy it while you can,
life is not a rehearsal.

Until your time approaches,
and in the face of that reality,
you may want to hedge your bets
just in case He is, after all,
waiting.

Meek. Mild. As if.[21]

'Make Jesus Che,'
the campaign cried. *
So, the posters went up,
and the people sighed.
"You've stolen our gentle Jesus,
all meek and mild,
and made him a revolutionary."

"Sacrilegious" they cried,
for they were very riled.
"Blasphemous,"
that Jesus had been defiled.
"A travesty."
The political elite went wild.

But then conservative church-folk specialise
in making young people feel neutralized.

"Political acts can be theological,"
we beguiled.
Remember that Jesus and Che
were both profiled:
they challenged authority,
were young,
idealists,
angry,
fought for change,
sided with the poor,
died for what they believed in,

21. The 1999 Easter campaign by the Churches Advertising Network in the UK, showed the famous Alberto Korda poster of Che Guevara with his beret replaced by a crown of thorns, with the intention of showing Jesus as a revolutionary.

had no option but rebel,
and judged by the powerful
to be criminal.

Jesus was crowned with thorns
not for being meek and mild
as Sunday School teachers say,
but for proclaiming the Kingdom of God
and show his people The Way.
A political reign of kindness, justice and peace,
The end of human hostility,
where people would live in true community
and Che's violence becomes Christ's tranquility.

The meek shall inherit the earth after all.

PART V

Church and Ministry

Believers in Exile

I have been forced into exile.
It is not a voluntary action,
but a forced dislocation into an unknown world
with no promise of a safe return
or arrival at some future safe mooring.

Like the Jews, I wonder how I will again
"Sing the Lord's song in a foreign land"?
Like them, I am in exile.
My faith is floundering in a world where
God has gone.
His old meaning lost in this single-tiered universe
with no Heaven for him to hide in
or clouds to cover his face,
as he scatters his Divine interventions.

My faith becomes an irrelevant side-note
in the light of Christian thinking,
as Newton, Darwin, Freud, and Einstein
enter our consciousness
and shuts God out of our closed existence.
Suddenly he is not out there in the sky after all
to be met after death if we have been good.

As the Jews could not return to the old days and the old ways,
neither can believers in exile pretend
our postmodern world doesn't exist.
We are in exile in a new land
and believers in exile face the death of the old God,
which may not be the death of God at all

but rather an opportunity to ask will he now grow
or die.

(Acknowledgments to Jack Spong for the title.)

They Have a Funny Way of Showing It

They have a funny way of showing it,
Christians in church, of being Christian,
of loving God
and their neighbor as themselves.
Nasty.
Gossiping.
Critical.
Vindictive.
Playing God, being in control, wanting their own way.
Racist.
Sexist.
Homophobic.
Misogynistic.
Pointing to the scruffy young new-comers from the estate,
arriving a little late for the first hymn,
"We don't want people like that in our church!"
is their mantra.

They are nothing like Christ at all,
these church Christians.

"Make them Christians," the Bishop tells his clergy.
But he doesn't say to start with those in church,
where they are barely Christian,
not very civil
and quite toxic,
often to each other in their mindless important committees.
Forgiveness.
Tolerance.
Understanding.
Compassion.
Words that get erased from their vocabulary.

"Don't bring the children if they make a noise," they say.
Their acid looks at a crying baby.

Are they trying to be Christlike?
Or do they think they have arrived?
And are saved?

"Disgusted of Leamington Spa"
is often a Christian.

Market Share[22]

A business selling products that customers reject goes bust.
Churches selling theology that nobody believes go into decline.
First, they start to flatline, then they bite the dust.

If the product we are selling is not desirable,
we explore why the product isn't viable.
So we look at the packaging,
and why it is discouraging
to the customer who finds it unappealing,
as their interest is revealing
that something else is preferred.

At this point, we change the product,
for something new,
for all businesses constantly review
their goods, to renew market share
by checking their product does compare
with others of a higher value.

Except, of course, for the church.
Which recycles old products,[23]
hoping that no-one will notice
that under the new packaging,
is the same old tired product:
a literal Bible,
stifling dogma,
anti-women,
anti-gay,
anti-lesbian,

---

22. Question posed to the JWT advertising agency in London, "How to market the Church of England?" Answer: "Change the product."

23. "Why Christianity must change—or die," Bishop Jack Spong.

anti-a lot of things,
including,
no sex if not married.

Attempting to uphold standards,
while hypocritically ignoring its own failings and priests still abuse children,
while only sixteen people make it to church each week,
closing minds to what they hear.

Does the church really know what its product is,
and if it does, why aren't the customers wanting to buy?

You don't package love with judgment.

Safety First

Supermarkets open and garden centers thrive
but try and access God's house,
and you won't get inside

No government forced the bishop's hand,
but safeguarding panic made them command
courageous clergy to lock away the key,
in case someone prayed too close to others,
and sadly passed away.

Social isolation is nothing new to Betjeman's country churches.
Every Sunday only a few come to witness
and sit lonely in pews made for closeness,
which now gather only dust,
and droppings from bats,
which caused the problem in the first place.

A golden opportunity missed,
to minister to a nation in loss, grief, and anxiety
needing comfort and care,
not rejection with doors shut in faces,
and arguments about how difficult it is to keep a church clean.
As if a bishop knows about this,
our Holy dusters could show him how.

Apostles were martyred standing up for Christ.
Safeguarding issues obviously more terrifying to today's church
than the Romans were to the apostles.

Baptism

Robed in white the new-born smiles in his innocence
and proud parents glance across the font
at delighted godparents in their Sunday best,
while Grandma does her best to squeeze up to the front,
trying not to bump into the candles,
as the vicar piously intones the church's holy liturgy:
"To be cleansed and delivered from all sin."

"What did he just say? Delivered from 'sin,'
What a horrid word. Makes him sound bad, wicked, evil,
not unsullied by life, pristine and chaste, and angelic.
How can he be sinful and fallen?"
Affronted and annoyed,
the mother nudges her husband in the ribs and starts to cry.

Somebody wasn't listening to the baptism preparation class.
In the excitement of mixing with the other new mums and dads,
they missed the bit with the teaching of the church.

The rules, the orthodoxy, the doctrine of the faith:
"The cosmic descent of man from a Divine creator still contaminates
with sin, all children born today who will lead a life corrupted
by Adam's fall unless rescued by a supernatural deed
which will free him from that original sin."

Or, as the vicar said,
"To be cleansed and delivered from all sin."
Stifling her tears, Mother whispers:
"But we came to join the church family. Lovely people. Welcoming.
We wanted him to be a God-bearer, to share in the Being of God,
loving like Jesus, not to be told he's corrupt and needs saving.
He's an innocent little baby, not a criminal."

By which time the vicar has reached:
"You have forgiven them all their sins,"
and everybody else is thinking it is about time
the church ditched all this theistic language
and produced a baptism service that emphasizes the accepting love of Jesus
and not that of a judgmental God with a long memory.

Where Have All the Churches Gone?

In times gone past,
we used to ask
where all the flowers had gone?

Now time has passed,
and the church's task
is to ask the same of the people.

Will they never learn
that shopping is no substitute,
for time spent under the steeple?

The young boys who spend their time
on Sunday playing football,
fail to see the game
will be their spiritual downfall.

The young girls cling to their phones
with a social media focus,
which give them overtones
of celebrity status.

The adults should know better
with years of wisdom to inform,
but we know where they've gone
—any port but a church in a storm.

Now we have to ask,
where all the churches have gone?
But we know the answer is,
they find it hard to carry on
in times when it all seems irrelevant to the people.

Too Much Evensong

My brain hurts
because I've been to Evensong,
where right at the start
I have to ask God to
"have mercy on me, a miserable sinner."
That's why my brain hurts,
as my prefrontal functioning
has been disrupted
and my amygdala disturbed
by implied criticism
from my Father
in Heaven,
who is supposed to love me
not negatively impact my sense of self-worth
by calling me a sinner
and making me feel neurotic
over how I lead my life.
Whereas I would much rather
have a shot of dopamine
from my hypothalamus
to make my neural pathways
motivated and positive,
not depressed
thanks to a church that rules
by making me feel
a failure—
not quite good enough.
Not perfect at all, like my Father in heaven
starting from the days of original sin
and labeling me a "troublemaker,"
when I challenge what they tell me
Little wonder that Martin Luther

was bipolar, depressed, and melancholy
when trying to reform the church—
too much Evensong, perhaps?

Millennials Leaving 2020[24]

I read recently of a millennial
who was giving up on church,
because she had a new way of looking at things,
which was different from the older generation
she found in a church who seem to fear her new ideas.

She struggles with the hypocrisy
of Christians who appeared "godly" with their
care for the homeless and serving others,
while neglecting their spouses
and criticizing their children
or watching porn.

She struggles with inequality of the church
and the lack of diversity
only just being addressed
after two thousand years,
as she looks at the top of most Christian churches
to try and find
spiritually gifted women
or people of color
or LGBTQ people.

She struggles with being told that
those of other faiths or none will burn in Hell,
which is not good when you grow up
and realize they are talking about
your Buddhist aunt,
your atheist best friend,
or your universalist grandma

24. With grateful thanks to Anna Dimmel, USA, whose sanity was saved by trading fasting and prayer for chocolate and honesty.

or parent
or child,
then hell is not such a good idea.

She struggles with being told that
the Bible is inerrant and infallible,
rather than contradictory
and not as clear as a Sunday School teaching,
but is complex
and we can disagree with each other.

She now finds a church in her home,
where all are welcome,
where she loves whoever she is with,
where the Spirit is ever-present,
and is waiting for the church
to embrace the same
before she can return.

Perhaps the church needs to
hear the millennial story
before it's too late
and face the fact that,
"Many people who love Jesus simply can't stand church."

Safeguarding

The other side of the coin
often points to a conflict.
Hate is often the other side
of the coin of Love.
Safeguarding is a good thing
when it prevents horrid unspeakable things from happening.
Safeguarding, going over-the-top is not a good thing at all.

Odd that we've abandoned the "jargon" of the BCP
in the good old C of E,
but have taken on the verbiage of "safeguarding,"
where the worst is expected of people
and little old ladies
and retired admirals
are expected to report their neighbor's
overloud voices raised at night
or enthusiastic sermons that might offend
the secure minds of blissful ignorance.

Failing to inspire worshippers
and ignoring the decline in congregations,
the church turns its attention
to bullying volunteers
who must tick all the boxes
or not be allowed to count the cash
or play the organ or ring the bells,
in case it gets in the way
of keeping their eyes out for the wicked.

The term "shooting in the foot" comes to mind
and another nail is added to the coffin
of the established church,

where good folk have had enough
and no one else is coming to fill their places.

Don't let them know that Jesus
welcomed the little children
whatever you do,
he wasn't checked by the system.

Kama Sutra[25]

The bishops today seem to believe
that sex before marriage is wrong.

Were Adam and Eve married
or just in a civil partnership?
If not married, they were a bad example
for the rest of us, from day one.

It is a long jump from disobedience
to "sex is sinful."
Judaism and Islam may have got it right
in leaving Original Sin to Christians.

Some religions have sex and fertility,
as central to their beliefs
and encourage consensual sex between adults,
regardless of gender.

Which is not helpful for us,
as an active sex life
helps you live longer, sleep better,
releases stress, and boosts immunity,
and makes for a healthier heart.

Time enough surely, for the bishops
and God,
to have got over it.

The rest of the world has.

25. February 2020, Anglican Bishops issue directive that for unmarried couples sex is sinful.

Taken for Granted

Some folks are just too good for their church.
Walking warily down wintry lanes
on dripping wet, dark December days,
to pray and to get to know God better.

Breathing through ancient lungs
because they are getting older,
the dust of generations
weekly disturbed by the holy polishers.

They return week after week
to their familiar pews,
having left carpeted and centrally heated homes
wearing warm scarves and heavy coats
to face and fend off the icy air within.

Caring and praying folk,
hoping and wanting the best
in loving Jesus
but shortchanged
with painful music yet again
as they strive to make a good sound
from the theology of hymns
of the seventeenth century,
to please the wooden angels,
spying disinterestedly from the oaken rafters.

Subjected to inane Sunday School sermons
about being good
from evangelical pulpits
and the occasional uninspiring charity visitor,
they never lose hope

that this week, maybe,
they may hear something meaty
to get their teeth into.
Something challenging and controversial,
about the meaning behind the miracles perhaps,
which stands a chance of being remembered
for more than the time it takes to walk down the church path,
on the way home.

They deserve better
but still, they come
to face ineffective, droning prayers,
which they heard last week
but haven't changed
and the hurricane continues to inflict its damage
on innocent California,
while Susan's baby still lies ill in hospital.

Wondering about how
a sip of wine and a bite of wafer
makes you a better person,
they shuffle up the aisle,
a chain gang of holiness.

And hope springs eternal
for folk who are just too good for their church
and deserve better,
patiently wait for revival and restoration
and an inspiring priest
who will halt the decline before they die
and their soul is no longer in need,
freed eternally from worship.

Corhampton Church, Hampshire 1020–2020

"Jesus said to him, 'Feed my sheep.'"
—John 21.17

Routed by the Romans who invaded first
British shores were safe until the Romans fell,
and Saxons ruled for 600 years. These warlike, pagan Germans
from nearby Europe before Augustine civilizes with the naive promise
that the Christian God will bring battle victory.

Then people of the Seax brave Solent seas
and carry stone home to ancient Carmeonton mound,
where the giant ancient yew sacred to Druids,
as a symbol of death and resurrection,
held their dead securely in the grave by roots entwined through eyes.
Yews, which suggest eternity to new Christians and conveniently provides
bows,
as well as cover for worship, as Romans appeal to pagan locals
who worshipped under the dark, berry-laden branches,
before they moved into their new church to focus on God.

For forty-six years after 1020, the Druid's gruesome eyes of death
revives through mists of time as Harold falls
before William's conquest quells the revolt,
destroys the art of the Seax and turn their nobles into serfs,
taking over church power and life in his victory
leaving Viking origins for Christian norms
still preaching the Word
reminding those on the edge of the swamp, that
"Jesus said to him, "Feed my sheep."'

So they continued to do so from a 3,500-year-old book
on a diet of a 2000-year-old theology in a cold 1,000-year-old building
until 2020[26] and now to a seventy-year-old people by sixty-year-old priests
still trying to save the message of the peoples from the past,
and all their time and effort in the face of the fact
that religions are born, grow and die,
and even before Jesus and Mohammed and Buddha,
Zoroaster claimed a supreme God
the faith of the mighty Persian Empire with millions of adherents
3,500 years old but now a dying faith
joining the myths and gods of ancient Egypt, Greece, and Rome
and significantly also the Norse legends.

Full circle back to the faithful peoples of Carmeonton,
still valiantly trying to feed his sheep
and struggling to accommodate a new mindset
that Christianity must change to survive,
while blind to the reality of the death of an inherited faith
that does more harm than good where God is declared dead
and his institution slowly declines
buckling under systems of corrupt power and self-preservation before the gospel
they celebrate with time-honored worship
and indomitably restore their holy place while they wring their hands
as villagers only remember a restored building
to hide their embarrassment at daring to name themselves "Christian,"
as the message fails again to make contact with them.

Unlike the Seax descendants,
they fail to comprehend the meaning of "resurrection."

26. Corhampton Saxon Church celebrated its millennium in 2020 with events decimated by lockdown.

Behemoth

The church lumbers on
like Behemoth,
as a Star Wars AT-AT
over every obstacle
trampling all in sight.

A church where Robinson, Cupitt, Jenkins, and others
merely scratch the surface,
of stopping its journey to decline
and Spong and Dawkins fall by the wayside,
as the Behemoth's roar
silences any contradiction.

And little children,
in their Sunday School innocence,
are taught to believe
the unbelievable,
which must be unchallenged
because a theologically illiterate teacher at
their desired C of E school also says it is,
through no fault of their own.

And in my wake,
after generations of false teaching,
lie the dead bodies of potential Christians,
of souls lost and of Truth gainsaid,
as the Devil gets the last laugh.

And Jesus still weeps.

God Saves the CofE

In the year 1603, Elizabeth I dies.

New King James lets his Protestant people
achieve their fervent ambition
of preserving their Church of England faith
free from Catholic intention to destroy
Henry's legacy of religion.

Catholic resistance still looms large.

The clues in a Norfolk church
provide evidence of Catholic intention
in a painting showing Armada intent
on invading and the blowing up of Parliament.

God then intervenes in both ploys.

His wind the fleet destroys
giving the Spanish no chance of firing a shot
and the gunpowder plot,
ends as Englishmen, inspired by the painting,
choose God's rule to evil intention.

Drake knew the wind was too strong
pursuing Spanish ships would be wrong
better play bowls on Plymouth Hoe
taking it slow and not rushing to sea headlong.

She said she had the body of a weak woman,
but Elizabeth sent Walsingham to be her spy-catcher
to make sure England stayed Protestant.
The painting's message is clear to all.

England may be in danger from Spain and Catholicism,
but God is on our side,
for which we can have great pride and hope.
God wanted us to win, and being ungodly and full of sin,
is a greater danger than upsetting a Pope.

So God is not a Catholic
and here's the proof:
He blew his wind and scattered the fleet
to the English God was on their side
and saved their C of E
by an Act of God!

Be More Like Jesus

"Be more like Jesus," our Bishop tells us.
So we tell them about him,
to get the ball rolling.
Comes down from heaven,
has a virgin mom, is a miracle worker.
But they didn't believe us
and didn't come to church.

So tell them to be more like Jesus, he said again.
So we tell them what Jesus expects,
say your prayers more, go to church more,
believe in your Father God,
have more faith, be perfect.
In other words, challenge them more.
But they didn't believe us
and still didn't come to church.

So tell them to be more like Jesus, he said yet again.
Remind them of the image we have of him,
passed down through the ages,
to help make us kind, caring, compassionate,
non-judgmental, inclusive, loving, forgiving, accepting, and tolerant.
But they didn't believe us,
and still didn't come to church.

So he told us it was us who had to be more like Jesus.
But we couldn't do it.
Found we were human
often got irritated, annoyed and angry
realized we weren't like Jesus at all,
too human and not at all Divine.
Even Bishops didn't behave like Jesus,

so what chance did we have
let alone the people,
who still don't come to church?

So how do we get people to come to church
if we can't show them, Jesus?

Navel Gazing

It is a reality to behold that
the Church of England favors looking in
over looking out.
The very last thing it wishes to do
is engage with reality.
Better by far to remain intent on living in an expired past
and formulate its ideology from the crumbling remnants of a bygone era.
Living on an ancient and medieval planet
being preferable to life in the real world
with everyone else.

This retrograde mindset being responsible
for the collapse of faith, worship, and
the general atmosphere of lostness and despair
which pervades the institution
and is chronicled in its decline,
numerically, clerically, financially, and morally.

Just a moment's pause to bravely glance into the Now of reality
would reveal the cause of its self-imposed demise.
University theology departments and theological colleges
have known and taught over post-war decades
the revelation of biblical criticism, academic interpretations of doctrine
and the impact of science on mindsets of belief.

It seems beyond the organizations' collective ability or desire to ask the question:
Why haven't the pew people been told?
The upside of failing to ask the question avoids the daunting downside possibility
of trying to provide an answer,
by correcting years of irrelevant teaching to the generation
lost to the church through disbelief.

Paradox

Our church life, its continued existence,
depends on people turning up
Sunday after Sunday,
week after week,
year after year.
At least it used to,
pre-pandemic.

Loyal and dedicated people,
reliable people,
the community of the faithful,
leaving their warm and comfortable homes
to travel through rain and snow;
to sit on hard wooden pews
often cold,
in bleak rural churches
with the sparrows chattering their indifference from the rood screen,
to worship and pray
to their God of love.

Why is it, I wonder
that through their shortcomings,
their misunderstandings
their petty mindedness,
their conviction of certainty,
their blind holding to the past,
their failure to read their Bible,
they constantly betray the Gospel,
through the ungodly behavior of the faithful?

Thor Returns, York Minster Burns

The Norse god, Thor, has been biding his time,
sitting it out in Asgard with Sif, his wife,
in their enormous house of 540 rooms,
waiting for a chance to use again Mjolnir
his mighty hammer, which throws out bolts of lightning,
which is what he does best and enjoys most.

Not the brightest of gods but the strongest
and very ill-tempered taking offense easily.
Thor rides out from Asgard in his chariot,
pulled by the mighty goats Tanngniost and Tanngrisnir.
Amongst the sparks and lightning from the wheels,
he flies across the skies
off down the years
to surprise Rebecca sitting quietly at home in Durham.[27]

"Your father has caused York Minster to be set ablaze by a lightning strike,"
they clamor to tell her.
"Not that, Thor again! And late, as usual, missed my father by two days! Typical!"
She replies.
Ignorant of Norse mythology
and oblivious to sarcasm, they are confounded
by Rebecca's refusal to take their superstitious charge seriously
because they really believe their god is jealous
and gets upset by current theology,
setting fire to churches to get his own back.

What sort of God do they believe in to make such a mind-boggling charge?

---

27. Lightning strikes York Minster on Sunday, July 8, 1984, two days after the consecration of Dr. David Jenkins as Bishop of Durham, seen by many as Divine disapproval of his appointment. Journalists besiege his daughter.

A God from past biblical times who sent lightning as a warning message may be,

along with blood, frogs, lice, boils, and locusts?

A God who sent a human son from the heavenly realm

to a virgin mother and who later performed fantastic miracles on earth?

A God of signs and certainties and past accomplishments?

A God so weak they have to defend him within the citadel of their own belief?

Could such a God possibly exist today?

Where is the God of creative risk for pilgrim searchers

who is above the differing rancorous trivia of his followers

and wishes them the fulfilment, contentment and joy offered them by Jesus,

and who doesn't set fire to churches?

Lanlivery Church, Cornwall

Spied by ships surging toward safety
in the ancient harbor of Fowey,
the limewashed granite tower of Lanlivery
stands sentinel,
and draws anxious sailors to a safe harbor,
before the long uphill trek
to worship where the Black Prince,
on route to Pelyn,
where thirteenth-century Kendalls tended his Restormel Castle,
had kneeled in days gone before
when this holy place, in Celtic "lan,"
was dedicated to a little-known Welsh saint,
a missionary "Liviri" by name,
whose predecessor St. Vorck
had found refuge in a north tower cell,
his holy work to fulfil
and watch over prominent Norman
resting in a stone coffin by the church gate,
who could no longer hear eight church bells
still bravely rung
calling the faithful to worship,
which millenniums later
pealed in glory at restoration celebration
rejoicing with great music and singing,
of English Heritage wealth
and restoration events funds
providing roof and walls,
carved bosses from the future king,
organ and chairs,
altar and font,
remembered by secret time capsule
from next door school now resting

below plaster in the north wall,
awaiting discovery in the year 3000,
while much-loved parishioners and priests
lie in dignified rest
overlooking the Fowey,
surrounded by bluebells and primroses,
campion and parsley,
in great waving and colorful profusion
awaiting the great event of the second coming
when the ultimate party can begin,
which will make it worthwhile
that they loved their Lanlivery Church of St. Brevita[28]
faithfully all these years.

28. Lanlivery Church of St. Brevita, in the Diocese of Truro, Cornwall, was saved from threats of closure through the activities of the "Lanlivery 2000" project and was fully restored in 1993 by the enthusiastic, hard work of parishioners and the largest grant ever given by English Heritage to a parish church. It remains a vibrant place of Christian worship.

Lanlivery . . . Our Parish

The past, present, and future of Lanlivery parish
is chronicled in its names.

There is a past to Lanlivery with its roots in ancient Briton.
It tells of bygone days and is Celtic in nature and name.
The Neolithic site here bears the name "Helman Tor" with its bronze age
remains
and from the summit, the path styled Forth an Syns
trails down to the parish church denominated St. Brevita,
lying amid Lanlivery Churchtown with its school of 1877,
an Inn, the Crown, of medieval longhouse construction,
the oft decorated Holy Well of St. Brevita
and then leads past the Sandy Way Cross,
beyond which lies the historic estate called Pelyn
associated with a wealth of eminent historical names,
William the Conqueror, Walter Kendall, Henry VIII, Queen Victoria.
Then there are more local names like Kendall, Littleton, Richards,
Pollard, and Higgs and Lobb,
Chapman, Wherry, Thomas
and Dunn, Dustow and Dyer,
as well as memories of loved names on gravestones recently carved
and still seen on reflection of past photographs of
the Home Guard protecting their village,
Lanlivery as "Ambridge" on Archers Day,
the great gathering of the whole village for V.E.Day,
everybody in church on January 1 for Lanlivery 2000
then across to the Crown Inn for the Millennium Toast,
planting the Millennium Stone in the church garden,
the unforgettable Saints Way Walk and Eric's Lanlivery Pageant,
with scenes from past times of the Neolithic, Saxon, Puritan, and Victorian,
culminating in the great Festival Week of 1993 in celebration of the church's
restoration.

There is a present-day to Lanlivery.
It is known in Feast and Rally and school events,
the Annual Pheasant Shoot,
Handbells at Christmas in homes lit by candlelight,
lively meetings of the WI,
awaiting The Granite Towers
or a Male Voice Choir visit from Polperro or Mevagissey.
The annual cycle of the church year keeps holy people busy,
Christmas and Easter and Ascension,
and the cycle of the seasons is a present wonder.
Spring flowers in the hedgerow, summer harvest and holidays,
Fall colors and wood chopping, winter snows.
Parish events and harvest suppers,
a flower festival,
bell ringers outings,
a visit from a Bishop.
Life of the Cornish households at Crift or Menawick,
Penarth or Streigh,
with others competing with the copious "T's" of
Tregarreg, Tregantle, Trethevey, and Trethew,
while at Colcerrow lays the largest lump of granite in the world.

There is a future for Lanlivery.
Telling us what's in store,
A time-capsule discovery in the church,
the aging of the Millennium stone.
Life at Churchtown,
growing children who will be the new life of the village,
changes in farming,
the unknown antics of grockles,
and maybe even activities of troublesome piskies,
and the ghost at Treganoon.
Forever the fifty-mile view from Helman Tor of Bodmin Moor, Dartmoor,
the Atlantic coast at Camel Estuary, China Clay works, Roche Rock, St. Agnes Beacon, St. Austell Bay

and always the Fowey River
gazed over by past parishioners resting in peace.

Lanlivery an illustrious past, a dynamic present and an auspicious future,
a proud place in history, of Christian worship and family life,
a good place to live.

Dew boz geno. God be with you.
Tereba nessa. Till next time.

Aquarius[29]

If the arrival of the Age of Aquarius,
with its new-age, pop-spirituality
achieves what Christianity,
and other world religions,
have botched
in the past 2000 years,
won't the church be annoyed,
miffed and generally hacked off.

29. We were promised this vision in 1968 in the London and Broadway musical
Hair written by Gerome Ragni and James Rado with music by Galt Macdermot.

Going Down with All Hands 2020

"Welcome to St. GoingNowhere's,
Just to let you know,
without exaggeration or hyperbole,
we are members of "The Flat Earth Society,"
committed to an ancient mindset
of no earthly interest to today's population.
This keeps us entrenched in the very church services
which put folk off in the first place,
which we call "tradition,"
but are really antediluvian practices
and credal statements
of an obsolescent and unsustainable theology,
to any reasonable and
scientifically educated person.
The language of which is still prehistoric,
despite myriad revisions,
and innumerous attempts to be
relevant, contemporary, and captivating,
which we freely admit we haven't achieved.
It's great to see you,
you'll have no problem socially isolating here.
Welcome to the lifeboat."

Kingship[30]

He is the head.
Not the bishop,
not the vicar,
not the church,
council or the people,
but Jesus Christ.

All are very welcome through the doors of his house.
When you come, forgive the human weakness
of the people you will find here.
It is Jesus Christ who waits to greet you.

Especially welcome are the little children, the sick, the lonely,
the unloved, the weak, the confused, the over-stressed,
the hurt, the worried, the anxious, the abandoned,
those whose friendships and marriages have broken,
those who are searching for more meaning,
and those who cannot understand these difficult times.
This is your home; Christ awaits your coming.

Also welcome are the proud, the arrogant, cynical, the critical,
the egocentric: those who are independent, those who are strong
and feel they need no help—don't kid yourself, your home is here also—
you must admit it eventually!

We will not ask for your money; we will not give you a job to do.
We will not ask you to hold a coffee morning to raise funds.
We will not ask you to restore a building.

30. Poster for my parish churches, 2000.

We will meet with Jesus Christ and worship God together.
We will meet each other's needs and understand each other.
We will shed the burden of all the pretense in our lives
and take the risk of being open and humble and vulnerable.

Bad for the Soul[31]

The Prayer Book tells Sally she's a "sinner,"
at Morning Prayer before her dinner.
Simon's "wicked" and a "miserable offender,"
and The Kingdom of God he cannot enter.
It makes Penny say sorry, ashamed failure,
for simply having human nature.

For Peter, a newcomer, this sunny morning,
this censure comes without warning,
and would make him not want to enter
if a judgmental God, he would encounter.

Our pre-frontal gyrus in our brain cortex
puts our minds in quite a vortex,
as neuronal action in this place
causes distress and a Fall from Grace.
Also, anxiety and depression,
and all before we make Confession.

But if in our left middle frontal cortex instead
positive thoughts could be spread,
our psyches feel joy and happiness
which makes us more likely want to witness
a God who loves us more,
and does not wish to keep score,
of our many failings.

31. From my letter to the *Church Times*, March 5, 2004, based on the neurological impact of the liturgy.

Why does the liturgy fail to see
we are evolving human beings,
try to be a little more accommodating
and offer us a service less humiliating,
mortifying and chastening?

And less damaging to our neural circuits?

PART VI

Culture and the Cosmos

Mother Love

Mommy, Child-bearer, Grandmother,
Mother figure, Mother's love, Mother Earth,
Mother Nature, Mother God, Heavenly Mother,
we have so many ways of looking at the love of mothers.

Our partners' happiness relies on it,
family life is built upon it,
evolution depends on it.

Mother love is unconditional and eternal and begins at conception.
Mother Church nourishes, nurtures, and protects the faithful.
Mary, Mother of the Church, loves her baby.

All of which raises a question
that must be asked,
and with which men must be tasked,
why women have been so oppressed
causing hurt and much distress,
for so long in a church
where compassion and care are fundamental,
and where the giving of love is the central message?

Shame on the men
hiding behind laws canonical,
and dubious theology,
to justify rejection
of those whose biological state
is not recognized.

For no adequate reason,
other than prejudice.

Turbulent Priest[32]

"Blessed are you when people revile you and persecute you
and utter all kinds of evil against you, falsely on my account.
Rejoice and be glad!"

Matthew 5:11

Presented by the rudest Bishop in the Church of England,
who has great humor and compassion behind the mask,
and who sees a glimpse of holiness,
and sends to Salisbury
for two years theological survival
before the journey starts,
for a fully paid-up member of the awkward squad,
and optimism and hope rule.

Soon there is conflict
apparent in this cradle of love.

Talking to glue-sniffers in the church porch,
is not done here at all,
especially by a naive new curate.
Supporting punk-rockers
unwanted in the church hall
and despised by the rector
leads to upsets and raised voices.
Lying down in the road
to stop the destruction of a Cornish village
with threats of arrest
ends in hassle in police HQ,
with churchwarden complicit.
'Jesus as Che' posters go up,

---

32. Autobiographical.

complaints come in from
non-churchgoing folk.

Outrageous "Beef on the Bone" and Blair countryside policies
cause face to face with anxious security teams
as hands hover over secret guns
through worry over the threat from rural peasants
and encourage defiant meal with a Lord's support,
and TV show to upset New Labour wishing for
showboating image.
Supporting the hunt on a rainswept day
with angry protests at the clerical blessing.

Buy African Bishop new car to travel vast diocese
with the cost of week's gin proving funds,
donated by parish
but sparking refusal to fill the black hole in the ground
with charity money as wealthy resentment grows.
Restore the church against Bishop's threats of closure
as EH come through with funds
and HRH supports
with beautiful wooden bosses to replace medieval losses
in Black Prince's church
overlooking misty Fowey in the distance.
Fireworks for clergy wife birthday
upsets neighbor's with complaints to a new bishop -
who wished for an invitation.

Adultery in tower challenged and removed
and stalking organist sent to play elsewhere
with front-page news
ruins good intentions of Christian effort
and Masons revenge
has final say
after retreating to a holy place.

Sheldon, Devon, a place of safety
for fragile clergy with toxic congregations
running down best efforts,
bullied by bishops,
with families harmed
and wives distressed.

Aristocrat patrons encourage a popular mindset
that clergy treated as a gardener
is the way to deal with an opinionated cleric.
Broken promises and bishop's lies
over job assurance
stress and destroy Vicarage life,
where vocal minority resent challenge to power
until Union rescue and tribunal vindication
admonishes guilty,
with parishioners on side to thwart power-mad minority
resulting in the closure of ranks,
and consolation price of an unwanted move,
when death and promotion sideways have the final say.

Well-qualified post as a hospice chaplain
dashed by episcopal intervention,
also even more qualified post as school chaplain,
raising thoughts that coincidence
is really enemy action.

Blacklisted by little men
with power.
Retirement blighted
and ministry refused
as harbored grudges take effect
on clerics trained to take as a role model
He who turned over tables,
upset those in authority,

challenged superiors,
head priests and the like.
He didn't mince words,
stood up for the weak,
challenged the lukewarm,
and faced the powerful
who didn't like the truth,
but who now want pliable people-pleasers,
weak and PC,
who don't rock boats,
and circle the honey pot with eyes on the big hat
and aspirations for the top.

And who cries,
"Will no one rid me of this turbulent priest?"
which must have spoilt Christmas 1170
for someone equally turbulent,
and his four knights.
And who is in good company,
for St. Francis of Assisi
and William Wilberforce
were both "holy irritants,"
in the religious structures of their day,
and even St. Paul, John Wesley, and Newman
had to take breaks and make needed changes.

Do they not read their Bibles,
before embarking on persecution?
"I say to you, love your enemies."
"If you do not forgive others, neither will your Father forgive your trespasses."
"Do not judge, so that you may not be judged."
"Why do you see the speck in your neighbor's eye, but do not notice the log in your own eye?"
"Forgive not seven times, but I tell you seventy-seven times."

Fat chance of that happening
in today's church of God.

Love is always a victim
when power is challenged
by weakness
and leads to a Cross.

"More Tea, Vicar?"

"More tea, Vicar?

What would you like to go with it,[33]
in your daily round of clerical life
where you are subjected to more than most
face at their daily work?
Although they think you have a cushy time
with your one-day a week working life.

Some PTSD or maybe a touch of GAD,
How about Mobbing combined with Chronic Stress
or Personal Criticism, Anxiety and Burnout
with Emotional Exhaustion and Depersonalization?

Not forgetting the High Demands,
Unrealistic expectations, Viciousness
and Toxic Controlling Congregations
on top of all the Harassment,
Conflict, Spiritual Abuse,
and Trauma.

No wonder you suffer from
Reduced Self-esteem, Suicidal Thoughts,

---

33. All conditions have been suffered by clergy in their work.
PTSD—Post Traumatic Stress Disorder. GAD—General Anxiety Disorder
CDM—Clergy Disciplinary Measure (2003); generally considered by clergy as "not fit for purpose." However, the C of E website's page on the CDM opens with this statement: "The Clergy Discipline Measure 2003 ('CDM') provides processes for dealing efficiently and fairly with formal complaints of serious misconduct against members of the clergy." After the Sheldon "Project CDM" was published in 2020, the House of Bishops voted for complete replacement of the CDM.

Sheldon (Devon, UK) is an open and welcoming community that is devoted to caring for distressed clergy affected by these issues. It is a wonderful place of retreat and a source of support, encouragement, and specialist care for people in ministry and their families.

Resulting in Sick Leave,
Forced Termination, Damaged Integrity,
Constant Worry,
and Family Stress, a Distressed Spouse,
and for many colleagues, Divorce.

Don't expect support from the top though,
archdeacons and bishops have better things to do.
Promises of care with no follow-up.
Best head to Sheldon where diocesan fanciful,
fictional pastoral care framework's
are a common theme,
and you find a wonderful source of support,
encouragement and advice
from equally burdened brethren and sisters.

Abandoned by the church and threats of CDM,
who can blame you for wanting to resign,
and have nothing more to do with it?
How tragically sad!
Wicked PCC's and bullying, power-crazed churchwardens
don't help, nor do malicious complaints made against you.
Little wonder your wife is distressed, your families' upset
and job threats loom.

Deskilled on arrival, despite your past experience,
with little hope of rescue on the episcopal front,
where safeguarding rules favor laity over priests,
you must muddle through as best you can.

Ministry is a high-risk occupation,
no question of that."

A Priest Is Sought[34]

Our church is . . .
Lively, energized, has huge potential, missionary, busy, active, vibrant,
impressive, significant, thriving, stunning, exciting, dynamic, expectant,
and hopeful. It is a "Benefice of the Future."

The priest we seek is . . .
Gifted, visionary, sensitive, enthusiastic, discerning, motivating, inspiring,
energetic, pioneering, experienced, compassionate, mission-focused,
empathic, socially confident, outgoing, encouraging, imaginative, wise,
creative, an accomplished communicator, a challenging priest—with a good
track record!
Who loves Jesus and seeks to please God.

We offer . . .
House for duty, lovely rural area, self-supporting,
but no money.

What about the quiet and prayerful and humble priests?
The burned-out ones?
The depressed and alcoholic and stressed ones?
The ones whose marriages are breaking?
The bullied ones?
The ones who upset bishops?
Don't they get a look in?
We don't see them in the ads.

What about the failing parishes, the not significant or vibrant parishes,
the "doing the best we can to keep the show on the road" parishes?
Don't they count?

34. With thanks to the *Church Times* job pages.

They want us to respect their traditional beliefs and practices,
but, at the same time, to develop new services to attract new people.
They want the sort of services which will fill the pews
with people who have no earthly reason to come to church
until now,
but will miraculously pour in when you arrive
and we offer them the service we,
and our last priest,
have been unable to devise
and which we secretly suspect doesn't exist
or the Church of England
wouldn't be in such a mess.

And if they don't,
remember
it will be your fault,
not ours.
In seven years you will see our ad again.
Nothing will have changed.

Nobody told them,
Archangel Gabriel isn't available.

No More Vicars

They say there will be no more vicars soon,
no one wants to do it.
Apparently, God has stopped calling them,
or maybe they've stopped listening?
Hands over ears and la-la-la-ing out that small, still voice.

Or perhaps He's just letting them grow up?
Simply running out of them,
like congregations and money.
Just handling decline but won't admit it.

Why would anyone do it anyway? Vicaring?
Tied cottage, like last centuries farm worker,
paid poor but behave posh.
Smiling viciousness as they show who's in control.
And finally,
to penny-pinching in small Basingstoke flat.

Lots of women vicars though, bound to be,
teaching pension and husband
with a good job and own house,
and Lady bishops as well,
competing with the men for a place in the Lords.

Gone are junior clergy.
Now we're middle management.
Loss of leadership, no new ideas,
just jeans and shorts, and messy church.
PC speak bishops with no theology
but pretend politicians.
Save me from a "safe pair of hands."

Like regional managers isolated from the shop floor of parishioners.
Admin and meetings and a computer screen
that demands no spiritual response.
"Think outside of the box," some chance.
Curate as the incumbent in two short years,
no wonder they burn out.
Mass redundancies may turn out a blessing in disguise.

Swing a child in Sunday school,
and safeguarding issues hove into view,
pervert or worse.

Why would you do it—vicaring?
To spend long weary hours
sitting, just sitting,
listening to the death rattle.
Again.
While thin walls barely mask mothers sobbing
and bustling relatives make yet more tea.
"More tea, Vicar?"
Screaming within, serene without,
as another one bites the dust.

Rolling News

TV news,
radio news,
newspaper news,
social media news,
24-hour news,
rolling news,
just rolling, rolling, rolling along,
in our minds,
in our faces,
of Adults,
of Children.

Presenters with solemn faces,
hinting at worse to come.
There is just no rest
from the bombardment of our neurons
by news—
mainly bad
depressing the nation,
filling all with anxiety,
so we think it normal to be
stressed anxious and depressed
when it isn't at all,
it's abnormal.

Whereas what God wants
and what we want,
is for us to be
happy.

Perhaps religion gets it right
with its daily, weekly and annual
demands of prayer
and worship
and holy book reading,
to remind us
to change
and habituate our neurons
for the better,
for happiness
and love.

Whereas rolling news
just reminds our brains
constantly,
and unconsciously,
to be unhappy.

Egomaniacal Me Me Me

In my world of self-obsession
I avoid all world religions,
and my self-infatuation
saves me from depression
by following the ambitions
of self-admiring,
celebrity traditions,
which allow me to focus on
my self-centered me,
and encourage my collections
of cars and jewels and well, me, me, me,
and not on the poor and needy
with their feeble mental health,
which other faiths all accept,
but my self-important me
is too conceited to agree
that they matter;
and my passion to be greedy
brings a revelation, blunt,
that I, I, I, I am my own religion,
and no PR stunt
will remove my self-interest in me,
I have a suspicion
that it may turn out unfortunate,
if I make an admission,
which is certainly very odd,
to discover in my atheism
I behave as if I'm god,
and my prayer is
"What's in it for egomaniacal me?"

Poems, Piety, and Psyche[35]

A poem is a piece of writing,
it expresses feelings and ideas,
its intensity in rhyme and rhythm
brings tough people to tears.

From the Latin and Greek we get *poema*
a fiction which poems create,
the French, *poeme* looks similar
which linguists enjoy to debate.

Old French in the sixteenth century,
gives us *piete*, and *pius* the Latin provide,
it tells us of being religious
and in some *reverence* resides.

Via Latin from the Greek, we get *psukhe*,
a difficult word to rhyme,
it means "breath, life, and soul" to the ancients,
we call it "soul, spirit or mind."

Rebellious Christian poets,
who mix faith and belief with the mind,
try to explore how people
in doctrine can often be blind,

when they switch off their critical factor,
and take old ideas as law,
and from rigid minds set in aspic
throw all modern views to the floor.

---

35. "Poems, Piety & Psyche" is the name of my one-man show, based on my life as rebellious priest and psychotherapist.

The fickleness of humanity
is worthy of study,
and can be very amusing
if we don't take ourselves too seriously,
as I'm sure, God doesn't.

Love Is A Funny Thing

Love is a funny thing
when you stop to think about it.

Sacrificial love.
Unconditional love.
Erotic love.
All you need is love.
Love makes the world go round.
Agape love.
Phileo love.
Storge love.
Ludus love.
Pragma love.
Philautia love.
Mania love.
Christ's love.
Love is an ocean of emotions.
God is love.
Romantic love.
You can't buy love.
Brotherly love.
Kill for love.
Love you from the bottom of my heart.
Family love.
Platonic love.
Teenage love
Love for "the one."
Love is where life is.
Unrequited love.
Obsessive love.
Committed love.
Better to have loved and lost.

Love is complicated.

Love is madness.

Selfish love.

Love isn't love until you give it away.

Die for love.

Love for a newborn.

Love for Mom

Love for Dad

Love is my religion.

Love is giving

I love you.

Same-sex love.

Undying love.

Love is blind.

Love will find a way.

Loved despite ourselves.

Lust love.

Love of Jesus.

Love is eternal.

Lovebirds.

Lovesick.

Don't' you just love it?

Love hurts.

Love songs.

True love.

Love a duck.

Burned at the Stake

Simply believe
the priest knows best.
It is not for you to question or think
you know better.

And if all is complete
in Father and Son,
how did they become three?

Why a third?
Unless to please those who like trios
like songwriters and sermon givers.
Simply believe, don't think,
the Truth is out there
like theological *X-Files*.
It will set you free.

The Greeks called a heretic *hairetikos*,
One able to choose.
They also called dogma "opinion,"
A different way of looking at it,
not an unbeliever at all.

All Christians should be heretics,
searchers after Truth,
only considered wrong
because they disagree with the accepted beliefs of the herd.
Biblical criticism, God's nature, female priests, and homosexual clergy
were all taboo once.

Not wishing to be burned at the stake of public opinion—
not for them the dangerous occupation of asking questions.
And why do these protectors of a loving God
hate others so much because they have different opinions?[36]

36. In Italy, the activity of the Papal States Inquisition continued until the mid-19th century. In 1908 the name of the Congregation became "The Sacred Congregation of the Holy Office," which in 1965 further changed to "Congregation for the Doctrine of the Faith," as retained to the present day. In the UK, on matters of doctrine, Anglicans without freehold can be dismissed by a Bishop through the Clergy Discipline Measure (CDM). In 1994, the Revd. Anthony Freeman was the first parish priest this century to be sacked for his theological views. In 2001 an Irish Anglican clergyman was called before an ecclesiastical court on charges of heresy for challenging traditional doctrine.

Homo Sapiens

Destroyed by Darwin
creation falls,
and we harbor doubts
that we aren't special.

Not a Divine image after all
but an accident of evolution,
in a universe still growing.

Unfinished.
Not perfect from which we can fall,
waiting for rescue
from meaningless sin.

God's intention is unfulfilled,
his effort was futile.
We need no Divine rescue
to restore us.

A higher consciousness not yet attained
awaits the painful passing of millennia.
Man's accomplishment proves superior.

And Eden's destiny is wasted.

Creed

"Jesus is Lord."

The original and best,
provoke the Romans,
enrage Caesar,
and put the Apostles to the test.

True Creed

"Jesus existed;
he was baptized by John the Baptist;
he was crucified under Pontius Pilate;
he suffered death and was buried."

Historical truth, biblical tracts,
even skeptics of Jesus can't deny the facts,
that this lot happened.

Nicene Creed

"He was crucified under Pontius Pilate;
he suffered death and was buried."

Metaphor, analogy, symbol, describe the rest
as believers attempt, to succeed,
in their quest,
for the historical Jesus,
as told in this Creed
which fortifies a narrative the gospel agreed,
which is a heavenly story,
but not history.

Creed for the Twenty-first Century

We believe in one God,
a name we give to Creation,
which nurtures the world
with maternal compassion,
and a father's power.

We believe in one God,
our teacher,
Adonai,
Jesus,
Divine being,
born among his people,
the poor and the sinful,
teaching and healing,
loving life,
bringing justice,
forgiving,
died on the cross,
our universal life force.

We believe in one God,
infinite spirit,
celestial deity,
higher power,
gifted to humanity,
to disturb and comfort,
who unified humankind,
and leads to peace.

We believe in one God,
Creator,
Emmanuel,
World Spirit,
Amen.

Opiate of the People

"The abolition of religion as the illusory happiness of the people is the demand for their real happiness. It is the opium of the people."
—*Karl Marx*

It's an unfair world,
where the rich get richer, and the poor get poorer.
All will be well though
after I die,
because I'm promised life,
up in the sky,
will make up for what I didn't have in this world.

Life after death makes an unfair world fair,
I'm promised a second chance,
when I get up there,
where wealth is just delayed,
and I won't have to share with the needy,
or poor aunts.

Many today fail to anticipate their fate,
no afterlife to look forward to,
no heavenly riches at the pearly gate,
while politicians take over God's role
in caring for his children,
little expecting their search for fairness
to become an obsession for greed,
and the loss of the people's souls.

Perhaps I am mistaken in thinking
that faith makes me happy,
when really all it does
is keep me locked into a world of illusion,
delusion and confusion.

The Religious Mind

"What were you before the world
made you what you are?"

A new-born baby perhaps,
before the influence and conditioning of
parents and school,
church and society;
of religious propaganda
and cultural influences;
of dogmatic brainwashing
and elitist education;
of nationalist expectations
and superstitions, influences, and pressures
over which you had no control.

You grew up being told
what to do,
what to think,
what to believe,
what to be.

Forced, without the option to resist,
into envy, fear, sorrow, greed, ambition,
you are now neurotic, depressed and anxious
and your mind is still not free.

Is it possible to be free from such subtle influences
and to see how they contaminate and shape and condition your mind,
influences which have happened in time,
and molded your unconscious
into the You, you don't want to be?

How then, to be free,
uncontaminated by what the priests say,
by what society says.
Free to be the You, you want to be.
Free to find God.

To be free from this.
You have to be alone,
aloneness where the mind
can find God beyond time,
for eternity is beyond time
beyond tradition
and accumulated knowledge,
and your experience of the past
where you were made to be what you are
but where you can now be still.

Still and quiet,
totally empty,
in the psychological time,
which is the *Now*,
where the past cannot contaminate
but can discover the eternal
and finally, become a true *religious* mind.

Sea of Faith[37]

How did it happen
that Christianity should rule so far, for so long,
before science and secularism disrupted religion
and reduced God to the manageable proportions of man?

Giant names challenge the status of the Almighty
as Galileo, Aristotle, Descartes,
Kant, Hegel, and Newton
with their new thinking dissolve the beliefs of years
and consign the dogma of tradition
to the melting pot of modern understanding.

When Matthew Arnold in 1860 tells of religion in decline,
he wrote of the *"melancholy, long, withdrawing roar"* of the Sea of Faith,[38]
putting yet another nail in the coffin of belief.
As religion frees itself from supernatural beliefs
and reveals its human origin.

The new thinking changes the shape of Christianity
but doesn't destroy it,
as it transforms into a spiritual path
to the meaning of life without dogma.

A path is being trod,
the declining sea of faith evolves slowly
into the sea of change.

37. Acknowledgments to Don Cupitt.
38. *Dover Beach*, Matthew Arnold.

Deconstruction

Taking the essentials of Christian doctrine apart
through postmodern eyes,
often feels like one of those cookery programs,
where modern chefs "deconstruct" a classic meal
into its various parts.

Eton Mess becomes méringue, strawberries, and cream
each in separate piles,
and Beef Wellington is a lonely steak alongside some pastry
with mashed mushrooms looking on.

For progressive Christians, Easter becomes the Divine touch of Jesus,
as the centerpiece on the plate,
with empty tombs, rolled away stones, and angels left as side-orders
from the menu of faith deconstruction.

Progressive Christians asking new questions,
thinking in new ways,
searching for the answers
mirror gourmets looking for new taste explosions,
which reflect modern demands for the "new cuisine,"
rather than the out of fashion food of the last trend
where past chefs expected their offerings
to stay on the menu permanently.

How much easier today's chefs find it to introduce new cuisine,
which modern diners eat with uncritical acceptance,
than it is for today's theologians
to get past modern Christian's stubborn persistence to stick with
the old fare of yesterday's ungodly menu.

Pleading in the Dark?

Robinson and Cupitt,
our heroes of the past,
had their preferment dashed,
now going nowhere fast.

Rogue Jack Spong they elevated,
the 'nightmare' in the States,
with his reputation trashed
he is the one they hate.

While Jenkins and Tom Wright
with the institution clashed,
their writing saved their day
as old traditions crashed.

Karen Armstrong stands alone
as a solitary female voice,
pleading for compassion
but her theology agrees with the boys.

Hans Kung and Marcus Borg
maintained the new tradition,
making progressive theology
an attractive proposition.

Now they are not alone
pleading in the dark,
as a critical mass of clergy now
on their quest embark.

To bring before all searchers
a new view of Christianity,

removing for the future
supernatural insanity.

A Christianity for today
motivates their intent,
leaving Richard Dawkins
to let his atheism vent.

Which leaves us with a question:
can congregations change
or will these prophetic voices
simply get estranged?

Stardust

Why are we here?
Where do we come from?
What is the point of it all?
Questions,
always questions
never answers.

Does our story start with the beginning of the Universe,
containing hundreds of billions of stars,
but no Garden of Eden in sight?

Question are we alone?
Maybe God made copies elsewhere,
or maybe we were the copy?
Did they get Jesus also,
or is he just ours?

Does our story start in deep space,
where the death of old stars
bring new life to the universe?

Starlight shines
and space probes prove,
that we are all stardust of
strontium red
sodium yellow
and copper blue.
Pretty but devoid of human essence.

Now I see the answer to
"Where did I come from?"
From quarks and joined matter and protons and neutrons,

building blocks from the big bang.
Where bits were assembled without out a Divine hand,
and 600 million tons of hydrogen burned per second
bringing light and heat to the earth,
and giving new meaning to *"Let there be light."*

A supernova expels life-forming carbon
and pretty but useless gold,
at the same time in the never-ending cycle
of death and rebirth.
Amino-acid building blocks make us children of the stars,
not of our heavenly father, after all.

The history of the universe resides in us all
and death returns us to the stars,
without answering,
"What is the point of it all?"

While the end product of evolution
remains a mystery,
and God's intention stays unknown.

Journey's End

The flow of time is forward not back
and drives the evolution of the universe,
measuring the birth and death of stars
as well as humanity,
making our future always different from our past.

And the physicists "Arrow of Time,"
compels our direction toward tomorrow,
as we cling to this fragment of space rock
trying to make sense of our lives,
with their pettiness and choices of TV shows,
vacations and partners, as if they are important.

Our sun illuminates the world today.
Until, one day, it just gives up and dies,
exploding our mortal remains into space,
ashes to ashes, space-dust to space-dust,
plunged into eternal night.

Leaving nothing behind but particles of light and black holes,
where past, present, and future are the same,
and only a sea of protons remains
where the cosmos once existed.

Resurrection and reincarnation may have been good explanations,
before science explained humankind's attempts
at the meaning of eternity.

Speak to me now of God.

Lost in Space

When the sun becomes a red giant
in eight billion years,
and our earth vaporizes
and it's too late to face our existential insignificance,
where will God be then?

Will he vaporize also,
as a construct of the human mind?
When there's no one left to name Him,
would He be gone?

Or will He still be out there,
somewhere?

Tardis

Yesterday, the past is not real
it's gone,
experiences only remain in my memory
wired into brain pathways
in what neuroscience calls,
"the remembered present."

Tomorrow, the future, is not real,
it exists
only as imagination,
and other simulated experiences
of the future
created by my brain.

Today, the present is not real
although it seems to be so,
as it ticks away hour by hour,
minute by minute,
as it records my life
second by second,
in which time light has traveled
millions of miles.

Only my brain and the Tardis can do time travel
and the Tardis is not real, but a TV creation,
whereas my brain is real and can think
both backward and forward in time,
but not in reality.

God has always been here and always will
"from the beginning to the end of time he can see everything,

and nothing is too marvelous for him."[39]
And Jesus is the same yesterday, today and forever,
whatever that means,
because entropy changes everything.

Even God?

---

39. *Ecclesiasticus 39.20.*

The Old Ones

There are more stars in the visible universe
than grains of sand on the earth.
We know who counts the stars,
I wonder who counted the sand?

Alpha Centauri,
the three nearest stars beyond the sun
likely to sustain planetary habitability,
gives scientific hope for life on other planets,
civilizations more advanced than ours[40]
out there in distant darkest space
reminding us that we are not
the exclusive justification for the universe,
but rather a transient component
burning briefly before fading away
unless, miraculously, we overcome
our historical human condition which drives us to self-destruction
and allows us to inhabit the galaxy perpetually
in peace.

If there are aliens out there
will they have their own gods,
or do we all share the same God?

Perhaps ours is only for planet Earth?

40. Carl Sagan called them the "Old Ones."

The God Squad—An Epic Poem[41]

The job of the God squad is to protect God
because they think he can't look after himself,
forgetting He is omnipotent, omnipresent and all those other Omnis,
which rather puts the God squad in their true insignificant and delusional
perspective,
of which they have no perception.

It is the God-squad's job to defend God against those who think
he likes homosexuals and can see no reason why
they should not marry and be happy like everybody else.
Obviously, the God squad needs to protect Him against people who think
like that.

They must also shield Him from women who think they can serve as His
priests,
as if such a thing were credible, and cause quite an uproar to make their
point
as they always do to prove theirs must be His authentic voice
because they shout loudest, and the loudest must be right.
The God squad is proficient in making colorful banners to help champion
His cause.

The God squad shelters Him from those who don't think He wrote the Bible
by directly dictating all those stories which were really actual and bona fide,
despite happening a very long while ago, and compelling them to believe
he made two people called Adam and Eve, who lived in a lovely garden.

---

41. This epic poem summarizes my perception of theology and the main themes of
this anthology.
"There is no God. How can he exist if he is reflected in a God squad that is so neu-
rotic, arbitrary, incredible, and demanding—and so completely out of touch with any
world in which ordinary individuals today have their being, pursue their hopes and die
their deaths?" Bishop David Jenkins, *The Calling of a Cuckoo.*

Members of the God squad, and there are a lot of them,
are sad that their God drowned everybody because he was cross,
but non-members must learn that God can do what he wants to do
and this just has to be accepted even if it makes no rational, scientific,
theological, or moral sense.

It is the God-given task of the God squad to preserve at all costs
all beliefs they know to be true, and to prevail upon non-members
to believe them also and see the error of their ways.

Even if it means persuading them . . .

Of the real *Virgin birth,* because Jesus didn't have a human father and Mary became pregnant by the Holy Spirit rather than by having sex like the rest of human females, rather than the more likely scenario that the biology of Jesus's birth isn't known or important as what matters is the inner meaning of his life that early Christians already knew about him. All we know about the whole Christmas story is that about 4BC he was born.

That at *Christmas,* a star stopped in the sky above where Jesus was born, angels sang in the skies, shepherds came to see the baby. Some wise men bought some presents unsuitable for a baby, and that the baby came down from heaven in some way, rather than the more likely scenario that the Christmas story means the baby grows into a man who Christians see as someone who brought meaning and love to the world, the rest of the story is just meant to reinforce his importance.

Miracles actually happened because it says so and Divine love can break the laws of nature, that's why sick people got better, multitudes can be fed with very little food, water can be turned into wine, the sea can be walked on, storms can be calmed, and the dead can be raised, rather than the more likely scenario that the physical happenings can be ignored as literal, historical events and seen as stories of "signs, wonders and mighty works," which presented Jesus as the special person they held him to be.

The *Resurrection* of Jesus shows he didn't die forever but came alive again after three days, even though we shall never know what happened to the body, and was seen as a living presence by his friends rather than the more likely scenario that the physical and psychological conditions don't really matter as he lives on in the present experience of Christians where death and time cannot destroy memories, or for the disciples after the event, the loving relationship they shared.

About the *Ascension*, as an ancient cosmology with an "up there," wherein a specified moment in time a physical body leaves the planets gravitational pull and 2000 years later is well on the way past Alpha Centauri making Jesus the first astronaut. Rather than the more likely scenario that the Ascension is meant to mean that Jesus is absolute sovereign and rules over everything, as in *"every knee should bow."* Still not a very universal doctrine in today's world, however, the church still getting it wrong.

The *Bible* tells the truth, it is the inerrant Word of God, and we must believe everything in it, even if some stories seem absurd like the world was created by God in six days of twenty-four hours; God made light before he makes the sun and stars, and then has a rest; Noah lives for 500 years; God drowns all living creatures (except those on the ark) to make the world less violent; the Sodomites want to have sex with angels; God turns Lot's wife into a pillar of salt; God and Moses talk through a bush that is on fire; trees talk to each other; Jonah lives in a fish for three days, and if you believe in Jesus you also will be able to do miracles, rather than the more likely scenario that the Bible is a man-made literary marvel full of stories, myths, symbols, metaphor, and allegory to explain what the writers wanted to tell their readers.

That Jesus was coming back any minute now for the *second time*, descending from the skies in a blaze of glory with a vast following of angels, to judge the world on his arrival. Rather than the more likely scenario that Christians wait for him to come into their lives every day through their spiritually felt connected to him. Not that he will knock on the door.

The doctrine of the *Trinity* actually does make sense. The incomprehensible trio of God the Father and God the Son, Jesus, and God the Holy Spirit simply transcends the world and can be wrapped up in the word "God," one reality, not three, a complex formula theologians have devised, rather than the more likely scenario that the doctrine of the Holy Trinity shouldn't be taught to children.

That *life after death* does happen, but eternal life is not survival or immortality or the resuscitation of flesh and blood or someone's psyche loitering in the background for a while or going to heaven, but rather more of a "here and now" experience of knowing God as Jesus and the Holy Spirit, which may help some but leaves most with not the slightest idea of what lies beyond the grave—rather than the more likely scenario that we all come from stardust at the creation of the universe and in trillions of years' stardust we become again. Ashes to ashes after all.

Hell is waiting for you if you are a doubter, of another religion, have any form of sexual relationship which isn't between a man and a woman, haven't been good enough and only true believers will go to heaven because only followers of Jesus are led to God and saved from hell, rather than the more likely scenario that there is no such place as hell except for when we lead our own lives in such a way it feels like being in hell.

That the *Holy Spirit* is not a ghost but the "reality of the unknown God" or the "ground of our being," the "third person of God" with no form, a "corporate reality" shared by everyone in the church, the *koinonia*, to which Christians owe obedience, rather than the more likely scenario that if we agree the old image of God must go, it is indisputably true the image of Spirit must go;

Angels exist and communicate with people in human form to let them know what God wants to say, rather than the more likely scenario that far from being creatures of fantasy they represent dreams and insights of a spiritual nature and for Christians stand for that sense of God's presence in ordinary life which produces the sensation of having a "guardian angel."

The God squad has a lot of members
because their God obviously needs a lot of sustaining and keeping alive
in these days of skepticism and doubt, disenchantment and unbelief
but sadly they miss the point
with their fundamentalist mindset that it all really happened as they tell
and they don't realize that without changing,
Christianity will die.

Lightning Source UK Ltd.
Milton Keynes UK
UKHW020926071120
372987UK00008B/250